PERFECT
PIES & TARTS

P·E·R·F·E·C·T
PIES & TARTS

DORLING KINDERSLEY
LONDON • NEW YORK • SYDNEY • MOSCOW

A DORLING KINDERSLEY BOOK

Created and Produced by
CARROLL & BROWN LIMITED
5 Lonsdale Road
London NW6 6RA

Editorial Director Jeni Wright
Editors Stella Vayne
Julia Alcock

Art Editor Lyndel Donaldson
Designers Alan Watt
Carmel O'Neill
Production Editor Wendy Rogers

First published in Great Britain in 1997
by Dorling Kindersley Limited
9 Henrietta Street, London WC2E 8PS

Previously published in 1994 under the title
Look & Cook Perfect Pies & Tarts

Copyright © 1994, 1997 Dorling Kindersley Limited
Text copyright © 1994, 1997 Anne Willan Inc.

Visit us on the World Wide Web at http://www.dk.com

A CIP catalogue record for this book is available
from the British Library

ISBN 0-7513-0489-1

Reproduced by Colourscan, Singapore
Printed and bound in Singapore by Star Standard

CONTENTS

PERFECT PIES & TARTS

Welcome to **Perfect Pies and Tarts**. This volume is designed to be the most informative cookbook you'll ever own. It is the closest I can come to sharing my techniques for cooking my own favourite recipes without actually being with you in the kitchen.

EQUIPMENT

Equipment and ingredients often determine whether or not you can cook a particular dish, so **Perfect Pies and Tarts** illustrates everything you need at the beginning of each recipe. You'll see at a glance how long a recipe takes to cook, how many servings it makes, what the finished dish looks like, and how much preparation can be done ahead. When you start to cook, you'll find the preparation and cooking are organized into easy-to-follow steps. Each stage has its own colour coding and everything is shown in photographs with brief text accompanying each step. You will never be in doubt as to what it is you are doing, why you are doing it, and how it should look.

INGREDIENTS

🍴 SERVES 4–6　🥄 WORK TIME 25–35 MINUTES　🍲 COOKING TIME 20–30 MINUTES

I've also included helpful hints and ideas under "Anne Says". These may list an alternative ingredient or piece of equipment, or explain the reason for using a certain method, or offer some advice on mastering a particular technique. Similarly, if there is a crucial stage in a recipe when things can go wrong, I've included some warnings called "Take Care".

Many of the photographs are annotated to pinpoint why certain pieces of equipment work best, or how food should look at the various stages of cooking. Because presentation is so important, there is a picture of the finished dish with serving suggestions at the end of each recipe.

Thanks to all this information, you can't go wrong. I'll be with you every step of the way. So please come with me into the kitchen to look, cook, and create some **Perfect Pies and Tarts**.

WHY PIES AND TARTS?

When is a pie a tart? A pie is often double crusted or top crusted. A tart is usually open. Much depends on national origin – pies, made with shortcrust and pie pastry, are British and American, while open-faced tarts, made with pâte sucrée and puff pastry, tend to be French. Whatever their origin, there's a pie or tart for every occasion.

RECIPE CHOICE

The wide choice of pastries and fillings for pies and tarts leads to an almost infinite variety of combinations. In this book are many of my favourites, chosen to allow you to master as many new techniques as possible. Plain rounds of dough are just a beginning – you will find pies, tarts, and tartlets in an exciting range of shapes and sizes. Some are international, such as Fig and Mulled Wine Tart from Italy and Plum Tart from Bavaria. Levels of difficulty range from simple Traditional Apple Pie or Classic Pecan Pie to more advanced puff pastry tartlets.

PIES AND TARTS

Blackberry and Apple Pie: fresh blackberries and apples have a natural affinity, and are combined in a traditional deep-dish pie. *Victorian Plum Pie:* a generous filling of purple plums and crunchy toasted walnuts bakes beneath a decorative lid of shortcrust pastry. *Cherry Tartlets:* in this Bavarian recipe, luscious cherries top a cream cheese filling, and are set in individual cases of sweet pastry. *Baked Cherry Tartlets:* soured cream and eggs are added to the cream cheese filling so that it puffs lightly around the succulent cherries during baking. *Lemon Meringue Pie:* a cloud of meringue crowns the tangy lemon curd filling of this enduringly popular pie. *Cranberry Meringue Pie:* bright red, sharp-tasting cranberries provide flavour and colour contrast to a topping of white Italian meringue. *Spirited Eggnog Tart:* the ingredients of eggnog, vanilla, nutmeg, and rum are added to a custard that is set in a crust made from ground or crushed Amaretti biscuits. *Irish Coffee Tartlets:* the hot after-dinner drink is transformed into a cold filling for tartlets topped with rosettes of Chantilly cream. *Rhubarb and Strawberry Pie:* the season for tender rhubarb and strawberries just coincides, leading to this double-crusted pie in which the fruit juices are lightly thickened with flour. *Traditional Apple Pie:* this classic pie is best served hot, perhaps with a scoop of ice cream or with a slice of Cheddar cheese. *Lemon Tart:* sweet orange softens the sharpness of lemon, with candied lemon slices as a fitting decoration. *Lime and Cardamom Tart:* rosettes of Chantilly cream mellow the tang of lime, while cardamom imparts exotic subtlety. *Pear Pie with Walnut Pastry:* wedges of pear are sandwiched between sweet walnut pastry in this speciality of central France. *Peach Pie with Walnut Pastry:* a pie for summer, when peaches are at their juicy best. *Chocolate Pye with a Crunchy Crust:* in this tart dating back to the eighteenth century, a velvety chocolate filling contrasts with a crisp almond crust. *Chocolate and Chestnut Pye with a Crunchy Crust:* nuggets of chestnut add texture to a rich chocolate cream filling, set in an almond crust. Delicate chocolate curls make the perfect finishing touch. *Chocolate Mint Pye with a Crunchy Crust:* fresh mint gives a refreshing highlight to the richness of the chocolate filling. *Strawberry Mousse Pie:* deep brown chocolate crust surrounds an airy pink filling, a cross between strawberry mousse and soufflé, highlighted by a decoration of strawberry fans. *Coconut Mousse Pie:* coconut milk and toasted shredded coconut are the ideal complement for a chocolate crust. *Amelia Simmons' Pumpkin Pie:* flavoured with black treacle, ground ginger, nutmeg, and mace, this recipe is inspired by the author of the first American cookbook, written in 1796. *Pumpkin Crunch Pie:* the pumpkin is spiced with ground

nutmeg, cinnamon, and allspice for this autumn favourite, then covered with a pecan topping.

Almond and Raspberry Tart: the Viennese speciality – *Linzertorte* – with buttery almond pastry, a dense filling of fresh raspberries, and a pretty pastry lattice. *Hazelnut and Apricot Tart:* sweet hazelnut pastry holds a chunky purée of dried apricots in a dessert tart that is perfect with coffee. *Plaited Three-Nut Pie:* decorative pastry plaits border a rich sweet filling of walnuts, hazelnuts, and almonds, bound with eggs and brown sugar. *Classic Pecan Pie:* the all-American dessert. *Caramelized Upside-Down Mango Tartlets:* in this contemporary version of the famous upside-down apple tart – *Tarte Tatin* – mango slices and caramel are combined under a sweet pastry lid, which becomes the base when the tartlets are turned out after baking. *Caramelized Upside-Down Peach Tart:* peaches are steeped in caramel in this spectacular upside-down tart. *Triple-Decker Dried Peach Tart:* when layers of pâte brisée and dried peaches are cut, an attractive striped slice is revealed. *Triple-Decker Prune Tart:* in this regional recipe from Gascony, prunes soaked in Armagnac are layered with pâte brisée. *Fresh Mincemeat Tart:* fresh apple and grapes are added to dried fruit for a light, up-to-date version of an old-fashioned favourite. *Festive Mincemeat Tart:* packed with dried fruit, this traditional Christmas tart deserves to be eaten throughout the year. *Flaky Pear Tartlets:* a sensational combination of golden puff pastry, warm caramelized pears, and Chantilly cream. *Flaky Apple Tartlets:* caramelized apples, buttery puff pastry, and whipped Chantilly cream guarantee approval. *Fig and Mulled Wine Tart:* cornmeal adds texture and taste to a pastry that is topped with lightened pastry cream and fresh figs poached in spiced red wine. *Fig and Mulled Wine Tartlets:* freeform cornmeal pastry rounds are topped with sliced fresh figs. *Mississippi Mud Pie:* this decadent dessert of coffee ice cream, rippled

with almond-studded fudge sauce, is set in a chocolate crumb crust, topped with whipped cream and almonds, and served with hot fudge sauce. *Gingernut Ice Cream Pie:* smooth ice cream, spiced with crystallized ginger and swirled with fudge sauce, is piled into a crisp gingernut crust. *Bavarian Plum Tart:* a quick version of buttery brioche makes an ideal container for juicy plums, baked in a light custard. *Bavarian Blueberry Tart:* plump, juicy blueberries, together with a light custard, complement the brioche crust. *Apple Jalousie:* fresh root ginger spices the apple filling of this French pastry with a slashed top that resembles the louvres of a shutter or *jalousie. Banana Shuttles:* bananas moistened with rum, then dipped in sugar, make a happy union with butter-rich puff pastry. *Hazelnut, Chocolate, and Orange Tart:* Italian sweet pastry dough is filled with a hazelnut, chocolate, and candied orange mixture, then finished with a chocolate glaze to guarantee that your meal ends on a special note. *Chocolate and Walnut Truffle Tart:* cocoa powder dusts the smooth chocolate glaze of this nutty tart, reminiscent of chocolate truffles. *Pistachio and Ricotta Phyllo Pie:* crisp, wafer-thin phyllo pastry encloses layers of pistachio nuts and lemon-flavoured ricotta cheese studded with raisins. *Poppy Seed Phyllo Pie:* ingredients from eastern Europe come together in a deliciously satisfying pie. *Fresh Fruit Tartlets:* a colourful combination of fresh fruit is displayed to perfection in flaky, crisp puff pastry shells lined with pastry cream. *Mixed Berry Tart:* an easy-to-serve band of puff pastry topped with Grand Marnier-flavoured pastry cream and a trio of fresh berries.

EQUIPMENT

The basis of all pies and tarts is pastry, and the most vital "tool" for making it is your hands. If your hands or the kitchen are warm, soak your hands briefly in cold water or chill the work surface by leaving a tray of ice cubes on top for a few minutes before you start. A plastic or metal pastry scraper combines the ingredients for pâte sucrée and pâte brisée with a minimum of handling, and the wires of a pastry blender cut butter and shortening into the flour for shortcrust pastry without warming the fat. A food processor is a useful alternative to your hands in pastry-making, and its use is also described and illustrated.

For shaping pastry you will need a rolling pin, and a knife to trim edges without crushing the layered structure of a delicate dough, such as puff pastry. A plain or fluted pastry wheel can do the job as well. With a pastry brush, it is easy to add an even layer of glaze to your dough and to coat tins and pie dishes with melted butter to prevent sticking.

To give pies and tarts the desired shape and ensure that they bake evenly and thoroughly, it is essential to use tins of the correct shape and size. These vary from French-style metal flan tins with removable bases to traditional heatproof glass pie dishes with sloping sides. Quiche dishes are often deeper, with fluted sides, and are made of china or porcelain. Note that the diameter of tins is normally measured at the widest point of the rim.

Speciality moulds include the oval deep pie dish for Blackberry and Apple Pie and Victorian Plum Pie, fluted individual brioche moulds for Cherry Tartlets and Baked Cherry Tartlets, and individual ovenproof baking dishes for Caramelized Upside-Down Mango Tartlets.

A heated heavy baking sheet under a pastry shell ensures that the pastry will be crisp. Dried beans or rice weight a pastry shell when it is baked "blind" without filling, so that it will not become soggy when filled. A wire rack allows air to circulate beneath a baked pie as it cools, thereby speeding cooling time, and helping a crisp base to stay crisp.

The range of equipment for making fillings encompasses everyday kitchen items, such as bowls, wooden spoons, a lemon squeezer, grater, chef's knife, small knife, vegetable peeler, and chopping board. You'll also need a whisk for whipping double cream and for making fillings, such as pastry cream. When making Italian meringue, you may like to use a sugar thermometer to check the temperature of sugar syrup, but a hand test is described in the relevant recipe. For making decorations with meringue and whipped cream, a piping bag fitted with a star nozzle is indispensable. As always, machines will speed and ease your work. A food processor or blender is useful for grinding nuts and puréeing fillings, and an electric mixer or beater is useful for making light-as-air meringue. An ice cream maker is needed for Mississippi Mud Pie and Gingernut Ice Cream Pie, and a coffee or spice grinder for Poppy Seed Phyllo Pie.

INGREDIENTS

The staple ingredients of pies and tarts are flour and butter. Because the final taste of the pastry is so important, I prefer to use unsalted butter for its superior flavour. In pie pastry dough, the fat used is white vegetable shortening, which contributes less taste than butter but has an agreeably light texture. In shortcrust pastry, the two fats are combined for the best of both worlds.

The flour used for all these recipes is unbleached plain flour. The gluten (which gives elasticity to dough) and moisture content of the flour may vary from batch to batch, so the amount of water or other liquid that you must add when mixing dough is always approximate. Egg yolks are added to the French pastries, pâte brisée and pâte sucrée, helping to bind the dough and give richness of flavour and colour.

In most sweet pastries, caster sugar is appropriate because its fine grains dissolve readily, leaving the pastry smooth. Note that a high proportion of sugar makes pastry dough much more difficult to handle, with the danger of scorching when the sugar starts to caramelize in the oven. Cocoa powder or finely ground nuts are other ingredients added to enrich doughs. You'll find cocoa powder in Strawberry Mousse Pie, walnuts in Pear Pie with Walnut Pastry, and an almond dough in Almond and Raspberry Tart. The freshness of nuts is important, particularly if you buy them already ground, because they can develop a rancid flavour when stale.

Fillings for pies and tarts must be full of character to contrast with the pastry background. Acidic fruit, such as lemons, rhubarb, and strawberries, are favourites. Less vivid fruit, like peaches, mangoes, and figs, often have caramel or spices, a dash of alcohol, and other pick-me-ups added. The texture is equally important, and here nuts come into their own, adding both flavour and a crunchy texture. Alternatively, a filling may be richly smooth with chocolate, cream, or cream cheese, or fluffy with whipped eggs. The ideas in this book are just a beginning.

BLACKBERRY AND APPLE PIE

 SERVES 4–6   WORK TIME 35–40 MINUTES* BAKING TIME 50–60 MINUTES

EQUIPMENT

 lemon squeezer

1 litre (1²/₃ pint) oval pie dish †

large metal spoon

pastry brush

sieve

bowls

pastry blender ‡

melon baller

pie funnel

chef's knife

2.5 cm (1 inch) round pastry cutter

vegetable peeler

small knife

rolling pin

metal skewer

chopping board

† shallow baking dish can also be used

‡ 2 round-bladed table knives can also be used

ANNE SAYS
"If you use a shallow dish, cut petal-shaped steam vents in the centre of the dough to let steam escape."

Blackberries and apples are a popular combination, ripening together as an early autumn treat. Traditionally, cooking apples are used, but here I use Granny Smith apples for their sweeter flavour. The pie is best served warm, with chilled double cream.

GETTING AHEAD
The shortcrust pastry dough can be made up to 2 days ahead and kept, tightly wrapped, in the refrigerator. The pie is best eaten the day it is baked.

plus 45 minutes chilling time

metric	SHOPPING LIST	imperial
500 g	blackberries	1 lb
875 g	Granny Smith apples	1³/₄ lb
1	lemon	1
150 g	caster sugar, more to taste	5 oz
	For the shortcrust pastry dough	
215 g	plain flour	7 oz
22.5 ml	caster sugar (optional)	1¹/₂ tbsp
1.25 ml	salt	¹/₄ tsp
45 g	white vegetable shortening	1¹/₂ oz
60 g	unsalted butter	2 oz
45–60 ml	cold water, more if needed	3–4 tbsp

INGREDIENTS

blackberries

Granny Smith apples

unsalted butter

vegetable shortening

plain flour

caster sugar

lemon

ANNE SAYS
"Frozen blackberries can also be used, provided they are drained of juice after they have been defrosted."

ORDER OF WORK

1 MAKE SHORTCRUST PASTRY DOUGH; PREPARE THE PIE FILLING

2 ASSEMBLE THE PIE

3 DECORATE AND BAKE THE PIE

1 MAKE SHORTCRUST PASTRY DOUGH; PREPARE THE PIE FILLING

2 Peel the apples with the vegetable peeler. Cut out the stalk and flower ends from each apple.

Apples should be unbruised, have unbroken flesh, and be free of insect damage

1 Make the shortcrust pastry dough (see box, page 12). While it is chilling, pick over the blackberries; wash them only if dirty. Squeeze the lemon and set the juice aside.

Minimum of apple flesh is removed with vegetable peeler

3 Halve 1 apple, and scoop out the core from each half with the melon baller. Repeat for the remaining apples.

4 Set 1 apple half, cut-side down, on the chopping board. Cut it lengthwise in half, then slice it crosswise into 6 equal chunks. Repeat for the remaining apple halves.

Toss apples with lemon juice and sugar first to avoid crushing blackberries

More sugar may be needed if fruit is very tart

5 Put the apples in a bowl. Add the lemon juice and all but 30 ml (2 tbsp) of the sugar; toss to combine. Reserve the 30 ml (2 tbsp) sugar.

6 Add the blackberries to the apple chunks and toss again lightly. Taste the fruit mixture, adding more sugar if necessary.

HOW TO MAKE SHORTCRUST PASTRY DOUGH

Shortcrust pastry dough is a sturdy flaky pastry that lends itself to a variety of pies and tarts. For a light dough, chill the shortening and butter, and handle the dough as little as possible. Shortcrust pastry dough can also be made in a food processor (see box, page 60).

Working fat with
pastry blender instead
of your fingers keeps
it cool

Work mixture to form
bean-sized pieces

1 Sift the flour, sugar, if using, and salt into a medium bowl.

2 Cut the chilled shortening and butter into pieces, and add to the flour mixture; then cut into the mixture with a pastry blender or with 2 round-bladed table knives.

3 Rub in the fat with your fingertips until the mixture forms coarse crumbs, lifting and crumbling to help aerate it.

4 Sprinkle the water over the mixture, 15 ml (1 tbsp) at a time, and mix with a fork.

! TAKE CARE !
Do not use too much water or the dough will be sticky and the pastry tough.

5 Continue mixing with the fork until the crumbs are moist enough to start sticking together.

ANNE SAYS
"The fork keeps the mixture cool and the fat from melting into the flour."

6 Press the dough lightly into a ball, wrap it tightly, and chill until firm, about 30 minutes.

Dough comes
together easily
to form soft, but
not sticky, ball

Handle dough
lightly at this
stage

2 ## ASSEMBLE THE PIE

1 Lightly flour the work surface. Roll out the dough, and trim to an oval 7.5 cm (3 inches) larger than the top of the pie dish. Reserve the trimmings.

2 Invert the pie dish onto the dough. Cut a 2 cm (³/₄ inch) strip from the edge of the dough, leaving an oval 4 cm (1½ inches) larger than the dish.

Use tip of small sharp knife

Sugar has drawn out juice from fruit

Pie funnel helps support crust and allows steam to escape through hole in centre

3 Set the pie dish, right-side up, on the work surface. Place the pie funnel in the centre of the pie dish and spoon the fruit around it.

ANNE SAYS
"*The fruit filling should be mounded in the dish; it will reduce during baking.*"

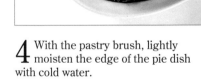

4 With the pastry brush, lightly moisten the edge of the pie dish with cold water.

5 Lift the strip from around the oval of dough and transfer it to the edge of the pie dish, pressing it down firmly.

Moistening with water helps seal dough strip to lid of dough

6 Trim the strip, if necessary, so that it is even with the edge of the pie dish, reserving any trimmings. Brush the strip with cold water.

Rolling pin is lightly floured so dough does not stick

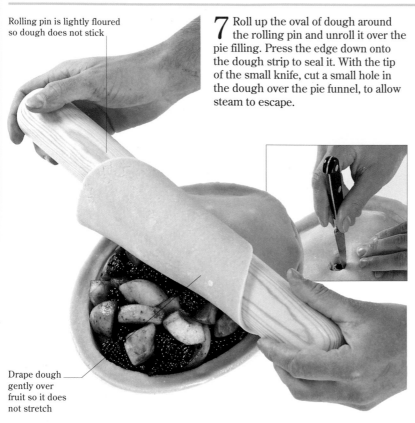

Drape dough gently over fruit so it does not stretch

7 Roll up the oval of dough around the rolling pin and unroll it over the pie filling. Press the edge down onto the dough strip to seal it. With the tip of the small knife, cut a small hole in the dough over the pie funnel, to allow steam to escape.

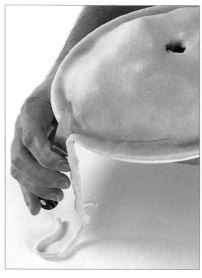

8 Trim the dough edge, lifting the dish on your hand. Reserve the trimmings to make leaves, flowers, and berries to decorate the pie.

3 DECORATE AND BAKE THE PIE

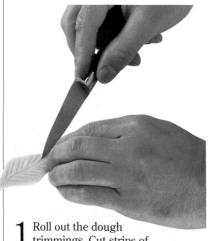

If dough becomes soft while shaping flowers, chill it for a few minutes

1 Roll out the dough trimmings. Cut strips of dough about 2.5 cm (1 inch) wide and cut into leaf shapes. Mark veins on 1 leaf with the back of the small knife, brush the base with cold water, and press it onto the pie centre, curving it with your fingers. Repeat, placing leaves around the pie centre and at each end.

2 To make 2 pastry flowers, stamp out 10 small rounds from the dough with the pastry cutter. Squeeze one edge of each round to thin it out a little. Set the rounds aside. With your fingertips, roll 2 small pieces of dough into 2.5 cm (1 inch) lengths to make the flower centres around which to wrap the pastry dough petals.

3 Wrap the thinned edge of 1 dough round around 1 flower centre, and pinch gently to make it stick to the centre. Slightly overlap the first round with a second round, and pinch to make it stick. Repeat with 3 more dough rounds so that there are 5 flower petals wrapped around the flower centre. Bend the petals outwards slightly to shape.

4 Trim the excess dough from the base of the flower. Brush the base with cold water and press it onto the leaves at one edge of the pie. Make a second flower and press it onto the leaves at the opposite edge.

5 For the berries, roll tiny balls of dough with your fingertips, brush with a little cold water, and press onto the pie in clusters. Chill the pie until firm, about 15 minutes. Meanwhile, heat the oven to 190°C (375°F, Gas 5).

6 Bake the pie in the heated oven until the pastry is lightly browned and crisp, and the apples are tender when pierced with the metal skewer, 50–60 minutes. Remove the pie from the oven and sprinkle immediately with the reserved sugar.

🍴 **TO SERVE**
Serve the pie hot or warm, with double cream as an accompaniment, if you like.

Fruit bakes in its own juices until tender under the golden pastry crust

A sprinkling of sugar after baking is the traditional finish

VARIATION

VICTORIAN PLUM PIE

This pie is named after the Victoria, a plum first planted in England in the nineteenth century.

1 Omit the apples and blackberries. Make and chill the dough as directed. Heat the oven to 180°C (350°F, Gas 4). Spread 125 g (4 oz) walnut pieces evenly on a baking sheet and toast in the heated oven until lightly browned, stirring occasionally so that they colour evenly, 8–10 minutes. Increase oven temperature to 190°C (375°F, Gas 5).

2 Halve and stone 1.15 kg (2½ lb) plums: with a small sharp knife, cut each plum in half, using the indentation on one side as a guide. Twist with both hands to loosen the plum halves, then pull them apart. If the flesh clings, loosen it from the plum stone with a knife. Scoop out the stone with the point of the knife and discard it. Repeat for the remaining plums.

3 In a bowl, combine the plums, toasted walnuts, and 100 g (3¼ oz) sugar; taste, and add more sugar, if you like. Assemble the pie as directed.

4 Roll out the dough trimmings. Cut out stalk and leaf shapes. Round the stalks by rolling them between your fingertips, brush with cold water, and press onto the pie. Use the back of the small knife to mark the leaves with long veins. Brush the base of each leaf with water, then gently curve and press onto the pastry stalks. Add a few dough berries, if you like. Bake the pie as directed. While the pie is still hot, sprinkle with 30 ml (2 tbsp) sugar.

CHERRY TARTLETS

🍽 SERVES 8 　🥣 WORK TIME 40–45 MINUTES* 　☕ BAKING TIME 20–25 MINUTES

EQUIPMENT

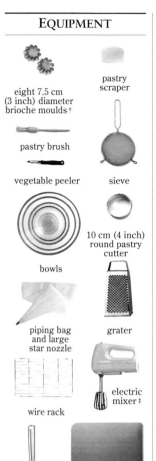

eight 7.5 cm (3 inch) diameter brioche moulds†

pastry scraper

pastry brush

vegetable peeler

sieve

bowls

10 cm (4 inch) round pastry cutter

grater

piping bag and large star nozzle

electric mixer‡

wire rack

small saucepan

baking sheet

greaseproof paper

rubber spatula

rolling pin

†tartlet tins can also be used
‡wooden spoon can also be used

INGREDIENTS

cherries

lemon

plain flour

cream cheese

egg yolks

unsalted butter

vanilla essence

caster sugar

redcurrant jelly

double cream

kirsch†　mint sprigs

†water can also be used

In this Bavarian recipe, cherries top a delicious cream cheese filling, set in pâte sucrée shells. Berries, such as raspberries, strawberries, or blueberries, can be substituted for the cherries.

GETTING AHEAD

The shells and filling can be prepared 1 day ahead. Keep shells in an airtight container and filling in the refrigerator. Assemble not more than 1–2 hours before serving.

*plus 1 hour chilling time

metric	SHOPPING LIST	imperial
375 g	cherries	12 oz
1	lemon	1
250 g	cream cheese	8 oz
45 ml	sugar	3 tbsp
2.5 ml	vanilla essence	½ tsp
125 ml	double cream	4 fl oz
8	small sprigs of fresh mint for decoration	8
For the pâte sucrée dough		
215 g	plain flour, more if needed	7 oz
90 g	unsalted butter, more for brioche moulds	3 oz
60 g	caster sugar	2 oz
2.5 ml	vanilla essence	½ tsp
1.25 ml	salt	¼ tsp
3	egg yolks	3
For the glaze		
75 ml	redcurrant jelly	2½ fl oz
15 ml	kirsch	1 tbsp

ORDER OF WORK

1 MAKE THE PATE SUCREE DOUGH; LINE AND BAKE THE TARTLET SHELLS BLIND

2 PREPARE THE CHERRIES AND MAKE THE FILLING

3 ASSEMBLE THE TARTLETS

1 MAKE THE PATE SUCREE DOUGH; LINE AND BAKE THE TARTLET SHELLS BLIND

1 Make and chill the pâte sucrée dough (see box, page 18). Melt the butter, then brush 4 of the brioche moulds with melted butter.

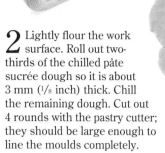

2 Lightly flour the work surface. Roll out two-thirds of the chilled pâte sucrée dough so it is about 3 mm (1/8 inch) thick. Chill the remaining dough. Cut out 4 rounds with the pastry cutter; they should be large enough to line the moulds completely.

Press cutter firmly to make neat edge

3 With your thumb, press 1 round well into the bottom and up the side of a mould to form a neat pastry shell. Repeat for the rest of the rounds. Add the dough trimmings to the remaining one-third dough.

4 Prick the bottom of each pastry shell with a fork to prevent air bubbles forming during baking. Chill the shells until firm, about 15 minutes. Heat the oven to 200°C (400°F, Gas 6). Put the baking sheet in the oven.

5 Carefully line each of the pastry shells with a second mould so that they keep their shape during baking.

6 Bake on the baking sheet in the heated oven until set and the rims start to brown, 6–8 minutes. Remove the lining moulds, and reduce the oven temperature to 190°C (375°F, Gas 5). Continue baking the shells until the dough is thoroughly cooked, 3–5 minutes longer.

Lift hot mould out carefully so pastry shell is not damaged

Shell should be firm and just starting to brown

7 Unmould and transfer each pastry shell to the wire rack to cool. Let the moulds cool. Roll out the remaining dough, line the moulds, chill, and bake 4 more pastry shells in the same way.

HOW TO MAKE PATE SUCREE DOUGH

The favourite French sweet pastry is pâte sucrée. The high proportion of sugar and egg yolks gives the dough a crumbly character, much like a biscuit. The dough can also be made in a food processor (see box, page 76).

1 Sift the flour onto the work surface and make a well in the centre. Pound the butter with the rolling pin to soften it.

2 Put the sugar, softened butter, vanilla essence, salt, and egg yolks into the well.

Well in flour is large enough for ingredients to be mixed easily

3 With your fingertips, work the ingredients in the well until thoroughly mixed.

4 Draw in the flour with the pastry scraper, then work the flour into the other ingredients with your fingers until coarse crumbs form.

5 With your fingers, press the crumbs firmly together to form a ball of dough. If the dough is sticky, work in a little more flour. Lightly flour the work surface.

6 Blend the dough by pushing it away from you with the heel of your hand, then gathering it up, until it is very smooth and peels away from the work surface, 1–2 minutes.

7 Shape the dough into a ball, wrap it tightly, and chill until firm, about 30 minutes.

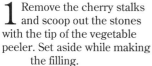

2 PREPARE THE CHERRIES AND MAKE THE FILLING

1 Remove the cherry stalks and scoop out the stones with the tip of the vegetable peeler. Set aside while making the filling.

Choose firm unblemished cherries

Point of vegetable peeler does least damage to cherry

Discard stalks as well as stones

2 Grate the zest from the lemon onto greaseproof paper, taking care not to grate into the bitter white pith.

ANNE SAYS
"Use a brush to remove the zest remaining on the grater."

Cream cheese softens quickly with electric mixer

3 With the electric mixer, beat the cream cheese until soft. Add the vanilla essence, sugar, and lemon zest to the cream cheese, and beat until light and fluffy, 2–3 minutes.

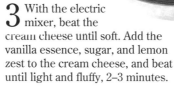

4 Pour the double cream into a chilled bowl and whip with the electric mixer until soft peaks form.

5 Add the whipped double cream to the cream cheese mixture and fold together with the rubber spatula until well mixed. Cover, and chill while making the glaze and glazing the tartlet shells.

3 ASSEMBLE THE TARTLETS

1 Make the redcurrant jelly glaze (see box, right). Brush the inside of each pastry shell with glaze.

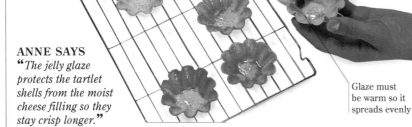

ANNE SAYS
"The jelly glaze protects the tartlet shells from the moist cheese filling so they stay crisp longer."

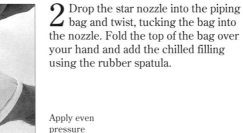

2 Drop the star nozzle into the piping bag and twist, tucking the bag into the nozzle. Fold the top of the bag over your hand and add the chilled filling using the rubber spatula.

Apply even pressure when piping

Glazed tartlet shells retain crispness

3 Twist the top of the bag until there is no air left in it. Hold the twisted top of the bag between your thumb and forefinger and squeeze the bag to pipe the filling into the tartlet shells, filling them three-quarters full with a rosette in the centre.

HOW TO MAKE A FRUIT JELLY OR JAM GLAZE

A jelly or jam glaze is brushed on fruit to make it glisten and keep it moist; it also adds flavour. Use redcurrant jelly as a glaze for red fruit; apricot jam for green and yellow fruit. A glaze can also be brushed in a pastry shell to keep the filling from making pastry soggy.

Put the jelly or jam in a small saucepan with water or other liquid. Heat gently, stirring occasionally, until the glaze is melted. Use the glaze while warm and easy to spread with a brush.

ANNE SAYS
"If using apricot jam, work the glaze through a sieve and melt again."

4 Arrange the cherries in a circle on top of the filling in each of the tartlet shells, leaving the rosette uncovered in the centre.

Glaze must be warm so it spreads evenly

VARIATION

BAKED CHERRY TARTLETS

In this version of Cherry Tartlets, soured cream and egg enrich a cherry-studded filling baked in the pastry shells.

5 Brush the cherries with the remaining glaze, making sure it does not drip onto the filling.

🍴 TO SERVE

Decorate each tartlet with a small mint sprig and transfer to a serving platter. Serve chilled or at room temperature.

1 Omit the double cream from the filling. Make and chill the pâte sucrée dough, cut dough rounds, and line 4 brioche moulds as directed. Chill, then line each pastry shell with a second mould as directed.

2 Bake the pastry shells blind as directed, 6–8 minutes. Unmould and cool as directed, and repeat for the remaining 4 shells. Reduce the oven temperature to 180°C (350°F, Gas 4).
3 Remove the stalks and stones from 375 g (12 oz) cherries as directed. Make the filling: beat 125 g (4 oz) cream cheese until soft; beat in 75 ml (2½ fl oz) soured cream, 1 egg, and 30 ml (2 tbsp) sugar with the lemon zest and vanilla essence.
4 Replace the pastry shells in the moulds. Spoon the filling into the shells, top with the cherries, and bake the tartlets in the heated oven until the filling is firm, 25–30 minutes. Let the tartlets cool to room temperature on the wire rack, then unmould them.
5 Serve the tartlets chilled or at room temperature, and dust the top of each tartlet with icing sugar just before serving.

Sweet pastry bakes to a biscuit-like crispness

Cream cheese filling offsets the juicy sweetness of cherries

LEMON MERINGUE PIE

 SERVES 6–8 WORK TIME 45–50 MINUTES* BAKING TIME 10–12 MINUTES**

EQUIPMENT

piping bag and large star nozzle

bowls, 1 metal

wire rack

23 cm (9 inch) pie dish

baking sheet

palette knife   electric mixer

kitchen scissors   wooden spoon

whisk

lemon squeezer   greaseproof paper

pastry brush   chef's knife

rolling pin

aluminium foil   grater

saucepans, 1 heavy-based

dried beans   medium sieve

small sieve

It is not surprising that lemon meringue pie has achieved international renown. Tart lemon curd crowned with sweet meringue peaks is a time-honoured combination that few can resist.

GETTING AHEAD

The pastry shell can be baked and the lemon curd made 1 day ahead. Keep the pastry shell in an airtight container and the curd covered in the refrigerator. Assemble the pie and grill the meringue up to 2 hours before serving.

*plus 45 minutes chilling
**plus 20–25 minutes baking blind

metric	SHOPPING LIST	imperial
5	lemons	5
3	egg yolks	3
2	eggs	2
125 g	unsalted butter, more for pie dish	4 oz
150 g	caster sugar	5 oz
For the pie pastry dough		
215 g	plain flour	7 oz
22.5 ml	caster sugar (optional)	1½ tbsp
1.25 ml	salt	¼ tsp
90 g	white vegetable shortening	3 oz
45–60 ml	cold water, more if needed	3–4 tbsp
For the Italian meringue		
100 g	caster sugar	3¼ oz
75 ml	water	2½ fl oz
3	egg whites	3

INGREDIENTS

egg yolks

caster sugar

plain flour

lemons

egg whites

eggs

unsalted butter   vegetable shortening

ORDER OF WORK

1 MAKE THE PIE PASTRY DOUGH; SHAPE THE PASTRY SHELL AND BAKE BLIND

2 MAKE THE LEMON CURD

3 MAKE THE ITALIAN MERINGUE AND FINISH THE PIE

1 MAKE THE PIE PASTRY DOUGH; SHAPE THE PASTRY SHELL AND BAKE BLIND

Use pie dish to measure dough

1 Make and chill the dough (see box, page 69), adding sugar, if using, with the flour. Brush the pie dish with melted butter. On a floured surface, roll dough into a round 5 cm (2 inches) larger than the dish.

2 Using the rolling pin, drape the dough over the dish.

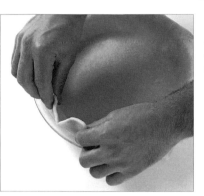

3 Gently lift the edge of the dough with your fingertips, and press it well into the bottom and up the side of the pie dish. Press to seal any cracks in the dough.

4 Using the kitchen scissors or a round-bladed table knife, trim the dough so that it extends 1 cm (³/₈ inch) out from the edge of the dish.

Pinch dough gently with your thumbs to make fluted edge

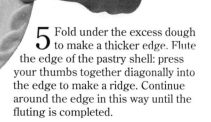

5 Fold under the excess dough to make a thicker edge. Flute the edge of the pastry shell: press your thumbs together diagonally into the edge to make a ridge. Continue around the edge in this way until the fluting is completed.

6 Prick the bottom of the pastry shell with a fork to prevent air bubbles forming during cooking. Chill until firm, about 15 minutes. Bake blind (see box, page 24). Leave the oven temperature at 190°C (375°F, Gas 5) and leave the baking sheet in the oven.

3553333333

33333333333

HOW TO BAKE A PASTRY SHELL BLIND

Shells are often partially baked, or completely baked, before a moist filling is added.

1 Heat the oven to 200°C (400°F, Gas 6). Heat a baking sheet in the oven. Line the pastry shell with a double thickness of foil, pushing well into the bottom. Half-fill with dried beans or rice. Bake on the baking sheet until set and the rim starts to brown, about 15 minutes.

2 Remove the foil and beans, and reduce oven temperature to 190°C (375°F, Gas 5). Bake, 5–10 minutes longer, or as directed.

3 Transfer the pastry shell to a wire rack and let cool before adding the filling.

2 MAKE THE LEMON CURD

1 Finely grate the zest from 2 of the lemons onto greaseproof paper. Set the zest aside.

ANNE SAYS
"Scrape off the lemon zest remaining on the grater."

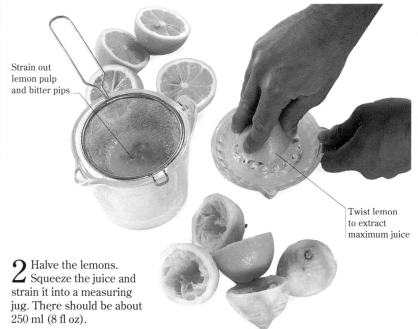

Strain out lemon pulp and bitter pips

Twist lemon to extract maximum juice

2 Halve the lemons. Squeeze the juice and strain it into a measuring jug. There should be about 250 ml (8 fl oz).

3 Beat the egg yolks with the whole eggs, using the whisk, until evenly mixed together. Cut the butter into small pieces.

4 Put the sugar, lemon zest, and butter into a medium heavy-based saucepan. Add the lemon juice. Whisk over fairly low heat until the sugar has dissolved, 2–3 minutes.

5 Off the heat, whisk in the beaten eggs until evenly combined with the lemon mixture.

6 Return to the heat and cook gently, so the curd thickens slowly and does not curdle, stirring constantly with the wooden spoon until it is thick enough to coat the back of the spoon, 4–6 minutes.

Blind-baked pastry shell will not become soggy when moist filling is added

8 Spoon the lemon curd into the prepared pastry shell. Bake on the baking sheet just until the mixture starts to set, 10–12 minutes. Transfer to the wire rack and let cool, then chill until adding the meringue. The curd will set further when cold.

7 Sieve the lemon curd into a bowl to remove any bits of egg or lemon zest, and set aside to cool.

3 MAKE THE ITALIAN MERINGUE AND FINISH THE PIE

2 Put the egg whites into a metal bowl and whisk with an electric mixer or by hand. Begin whisking slowly, but increase the speed when the egg whites become foamy and white. Continue whisking the egg whites until stiff peaks form when the beaters are lifted.

1 Heat the sugar in the water until dissolved. Boil, without stirring, until syrup reaches hard ball stage. Meanwhile, preparc to whisk the egg whites, so they are ready just when the syrup reaches hard ball stage. To test for hard ball stage (120°C/248°F on sugar thermometer), remove the syrup from the heat, take a small spoonful, and let cool, a few seconds. Take a little syrup between forefinger and thumb. It should form a firm, pliable ball.

Egg whites reach maximum volume when whisked in metal bowl

HOW TO FILL A PIPING BAG

Use a rubber spatula or pastry scraper when filling a piping bag with meringue or cream.

1 Drop a nozzle into a piping bag and twist, tucking the bag into the nozzle. This prevents the mixture from leaking.

2 Fold the top of the bag over your hand. Add the meringue or cream to be piped, pressing it down into the bag.

3 Twist the top of the bag until no air is left in it. To pipe, hold the twisted top of the bag between thumb and forefinger and squeeze the bag gently to press out the mixture. Do not squeeze the bag with your other hand, but use it to guide the nozzle as you pipe.

3 Gradually pour the hot sugar syrup into the beaten egg whites, beating constantly.

! TAKE CARE !
Be sure to pour the syrup directly into the egg whites so that it does not stick to the side of the bowl.

Damp tea towel under bowl keeps it from slipping

Beat constantly while pouring in hot sugar syrup

4 Continue beating the mixture until the meringue is cool and stiff, about 5 minutes.

5 Heat the grill. With the palette knife, spread half of the meringue over the filling to cover.

6 Put the remaining meringue into the piping bag fitted with the large star nozzle (see box, left). Pipe meringue decoration like the spokes of a wheel over the pie, finishing with a rosette in the centre.

Central rosette should be same height as surrounding meringue, so top browns evenly

7 Grill the pie 7.5 cm (3 inches) from the heat until the meringue is golden brown, 1–2 minutes.

ANNE SAYS
"Make sure that you grill the meringue at once so it does not start to separate and become sticky."

TO SERVE
Transfer the pie to a serving platter and serve from the pie dish while the meringue is warm and the filling is chilled. Cut it into wedges with a knife dipped in hot water to cut cleanly.

Fluted golden pastry edge looks appetizing

Piped meringue makes a mouthwatering finish

VARIATION
CRANBERRY MERINGUE PIE

In this colourful variation of Lemon Meringue Pie, bright red sour cranberries are simmered with sugar just until they pop and release their juices, then thickened with eggs. To add texture, the cranberry curd is left unsieved.

1 Omit the lemon curd. Make and chill the pie pastry dough; line the pie dish, scallop the pastry edge (see page 123), and bake the shell blind as directed.
2 Make the cranberry filling: beat 3 egg yolks with 3 whole eggs until mixed.

3 In a heavy-based saucepan, combine 150 g (5 oz) sugar, 250 g (8 oz) fresh cranberries, and 125 ml (4 fl oz) water. Simmer, stirring occasionally, just until the cranberries pop, 5–7 minutes. Lower the heat, and stir in 30 ml (2 tbsp) butter. Remove from the heat and whisk in the eggs. Continue cooking over low heat, stirring with a wooden spoon, until the curd is thick enough to coat the back of the spoon, 4–6 minutes. Let cool slightly.

4 Spoon the cranberry curd into the shell; bake, let cool, and chill as directed.
5 Make the Italian meringue as directed. With a palette knife, spread the meringue over the cranberry filling to cover it completely, mounding it well; then make decorative swirls in the meringue with the palette knife. Grill and serve the pie as directed.

SPIRITED EGGNOG TART

🍽 SERVES 6–8 🥄 **WORK TIME 40–45 MINUTES*** ❄ **SETTING TIME 2–3 HOURS**

EQUIPMENT

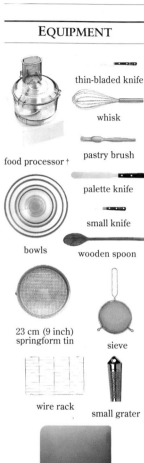

thin-bladed knife

whisk

pastry brush

food processor †

palette knife

small knife

bowls

wooden spoon

23 cm (9 inch) springform tin

sieve

wire rack

small grater

baking sheet

saucepans, 1 heavy-based with lid

rubber spatula

†rolling pin and plastic bag can also be used

Eggnog is a rich drink made with eggs and spirits. In this recipe, it is transformed into a creamy, rum-flavoured tart that is chilled, then topped with freshly grated nutmeg just before serving. The crust is made of almond-flavoured Amaretti biscuits, which are crushed to crumbs, then moistened with butter. Other types of crisp biscuit can also be used.

GETTING AHEAD

The tart can be made up to 1 day ahead and kept, covered, in the refrigerator. Add the nutmeg just before serving.

*plus 15 minutes chilling and 10–15 minutes baking blind

metric	SHOPPING LIST	imperial
500 ml	milk	16 fl oz
1	vanilla pod or 5 ml (1 tsp) vanilla essence	1
50 g	caster sugar	1 ¾ oz
30 ml	cornflour	2 tbsp
4	egg yolks	4
125 ml	double cream	4 fl oz
7 g	powdered gelatine	¼ oz
60 ml	dark rum, more to taste	2 fl oz
	whole nutmeg	
	For the Amaretti biscuit crust	
125 g	unsalted butter, more for springform tin	4 oz
250 g	Amaretti biscuits	8 oz

INGREDIENTS

egg yolks

milk

vanilla pod

dark rum

caster sugar

double cream

Amaretti biscuits

unsalted butter

powdered gelatine

whole nutmeg †

cornflour

† 1.25 ml (¼ tsp) ground nutmeg can also be used

ORDER OF WORK

1 MAKE AND BAKE THE AMARETTI BISCUIT CRUST

2 MAKE THE CUSTARD

3 FINISH THE FILLING; ASSEMBLE TART

1 MAKE AND BAKE THE AMARETTI BISCUIT CRUST

1 Heat the oven to 180°C (350°F, Gas 4). Melt the butter in a small saucepan. Brush the springform tin with melted butter. Grind the Amaretti biscuits to fine crumbs in the food processor. Alternatively, put them in a plastic bag and crush them with a rolling pin. Transfer the crumbs to a medium bowl.

2 Add the melted butter to the crumbs, and stir until all the crumbs are moistened.

3 Press the crumb mixture evenly over the bottom and 2.5 cm (1 inch) up the side of the tin. Chill until firm, about 15 minutes. Put the baking sheet in the oven to heat. Bake the crust on the heated baking sheet, 10–15 minutes. Let cool on the wire rack.

Use back of metal spoon to press crumb mixture into tin

2 MAKE THE CUSTARD

1 Put the milk in the heavy-based saucepan. Split the vanilla pod lengthwise in half and add it to the milk. Bring just to a boil, then remove from the heat, cover, and let stand in a warm place, 10–15 minutes. Remove the vanilla pod, rinse it, and store to use again.

2 Set aside one-quarter of the milk. Add the sugar to the remaining hot milk in the saucepan; stir until dissolved.

3 Put the cornflour and egg yolks in a medium bowl and whisk them together until smooth.

Pour sweetened milk in steady stream

4 Whisk the sweetened hot milk into the cornflour and egg yolk mixture, and continue to whisk just until the custard mixture is smooth.

5 Pour the mixture back into the heavy-based saucepan and cook over medium heat, stirring constantly with the wooden spoon, just until it comes to a boil and is thick enough to coat the back of the spoon. Your finger will leave a clear trail across the back of the spoon.

! TAKE CARE !
Do not continue to boil the custard or it may curdle.

Stir in figure-of-eight motion so custard does not scorch on bottom of pan

Bring custard just to a boil to cook egg yolks

6 Off the heat, stir the reserved milk into the custard and strain it into a cold bowl. Stir in the vanilla essence, if using. Cover tightly to prevent a skin forming on the surface of the custard and let cool to tepid.

3 FINISH THE FILLING; ASSEMBLE TART

1 Pour the cream into a chilled bowl and whip with the whisk until soft peaks form; cover and chill.

2 Sprinkle the gelatine evenly over the rum in a small saucepan. Let soak, 5 minutes. The gelatine will soften to a spongy consistency. Set pan over low heat and melt until pourable, shaking the pan occasionally, 1–2 minutes.

! TAKE CARE !
Do not stir gelatine, or it will become stringy or form lumps.

3 Stir the gelatine mixture into the tepid custard. Taste the custard, adding more rum, if you like.

Stir melted gelatine into warm custard, so they mix evenly

4 Set the bowl of custard in a larger bowl, half filled with iced water, and stir gently until the custard starts to thicken and set.

5 Remove the bowl of setting custard immediately from the bowl of iced water and whisk the custard briskly to lighten it, about 10 seconds.

6 Add the whipped cream to the custard and fold together gently, scooping under the custard and turning the mixture over. At the same time, turn the bowl anticlockwise.

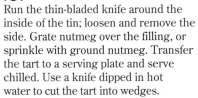

7 Pour the filling into the biscuit crust, smooth the top with the palette knife, if necessary, then chill the tart until set, 2–3 hours.

🍽 TO SERVE

Run the thin-bladed knife around the inside of the tin; loosen and remove the side. Grate nutmeg over the filling, or sprinkle with ground nutmeg. Transfer the tart to a serving plate and serve chilled. Use a knife dipped in hot water to cut the tart into wedges.

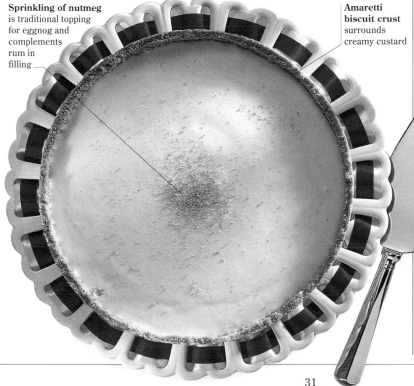

Sprinkling of nutmeg is traditional topping for eggnog and complements rum in filling

Amaretti biscuit crust surrounds creamy custard

VARIATION
IRISH COFFEE TARTLETS

Coffee and Irish whiskey flavour the custard in this variation, mimicking the beverage that is renowned in Ireland and internationally.

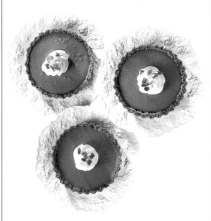

1 Omit the nutmeg, vanilla pod, and rum. Make double the quantity of the Amaretti biscuit crust, using 250 g (8 oz) unsalted butter and 500 g (1 lb) Amaretti biscuits. Press the mixture into eight 10 cm (4 inch) tartlet tins with removable bases, and chill and bake as directed, 8–10 minutes.

2 Make the custard: put the milk in a heavy-based saucepan with 45 ml (3 tbsp) instant coffee granules and bring just to a boil, stirring until coffee is dissolved. Finish the custard as directed. Finish the filling, using whiskey in place of rum. Assemble and chill the tartlets as directed.

3 Meanwhile, make Chantilly cream to decorate the tartlets: whip 175 ml (6 fl oz) double cream in a chilled bowl until soft peaks form. Add 10 ml (2 tsp) icing sugar, and 2.5 ml ($^1/_2$ tsp) vanilla essence; continue whipping until stiff peaks form. Chill.

4 Put the Chantilly cream into a piping bag, fitted with a star nozzle, and pipe a cream rosette on top of each tartlet. Decorate with brown sugar crystals, if you like. Serve within 2 hours.

RHUBARB AND STRAWBERRY PIE

 SERVES 6–8   WORK TIME 30–35 MINUTES*   BAKING TIME 50–55 MINUTES

EQUIPMENT

pastry brush

chef's knife

small knife

23 cm (9 inch)
pie dish

large metal spoon

grater

bowls

chopping
board

greaseproof paper

rolling pin

aluminium foil

sieve

metal skewer

baking sheet

wire rack

Tart rhubarb, one of the first fruits of spring, is united with sweet strawberries in this favourite pie, which is good warm or at room temperature. Pouring cream or ice cream would make a good accompaniment.

GETTING AHEAD

The pie pastry dough can be made up to 2 days ahead and kept, tightly wrapped, in the refrigerator. The pie is best the day it is baked.

*plus 1 hour chilling time

metric	SHOPPING LIST	imperial
1 kg	rhubarb	2 lb
375 g	strawberries	12 oz
1	orange	1
250 g	caster sugar	8 oz
1.25 ml	salt	1/4 tsp
30 g	plain flour	1 oz
15 ml	unsalted butter, more for pie dish	1 tbsp
For the pie pastry dough		
330 g	plain flour	11 oz
30 ml	caster sugar (optional)	2 tbsp
2.5 ml	salt	1/2 tsp
150 g	white vegetable shortening	5 oz
90–105 ml	cold water, more if needed	6–7 tbsp
For the glaze		
15 ml	milk	1 tbsp
15 ml	caster sugar	1 tbsp

INGREDIENTS

rhubarb

strawberries

plain flour

unsalted butter

orange

vegetable
shortening

caster
sugar

milk

ORDER OF WORK

1 MAKE THE PIE PASTRY DOUGH AND LINE THE PIE DISH

2 PREPARE THE FRUIT FILLING AND FILL THE PREPARED PASTRY SHELL

3 COVER, DECORATE, AND BAKE THE PIE

1 MAKE THE PIE PASTRY DOUGH AND LINE THE PIE DISH

Use quick strokes of knife to trim dough shell

1 Make and chill the dough (see box, page 69), adding the sugar, if using, with the flour. Brush the pie dish with melted butter. Lightly flour the work surface. Roll out two-thirds of the dough into a round 5 cm (2 inches) larger than the top of the dish. Using the rolling pin, drape dough over the dish.

2 Gently lift the edge of the dough with the fingertips of one hand, and press it well into the bottom and up the side of the pie dish with the fingertips of the other hand.

3 Lift the dish and trim the dough even with the outer edge of the dish, using a table knife. Reserve the trimmings. Chill the pastry shell until firm, about 15 minutes.

2 PREPARE THE FRUIT FILLING AND FILL THE PREPARED PASTRY SHELL

1 Trim the rhubarb stalks, wash, then drain them. Gather 2 or 3 stalks together at a time, and cut crosswise into 1.25 cm (¹/₂ inch) slices. Hull the strawberries, washing only if dirty. Halve or quarter them according to size.

Look for bright red crisp stalks when buying rhubarb

2 Using the medium grid of the grater, grate the zest from the orange onto greaseproof paper.

3 In a bowl, combine the rhubarb, orange zest, sugar, salt, and flour, and stir to mix. Add the strawberries and toss gently.

4 Spoon the fruit mixture into the lined pie dish, doming it slightly. Cut the butter into small pieces and dot the pieces over the filling.

Cubes of butter enrich filling

3 COVER, DECORATE, AND BAKE THE PIE

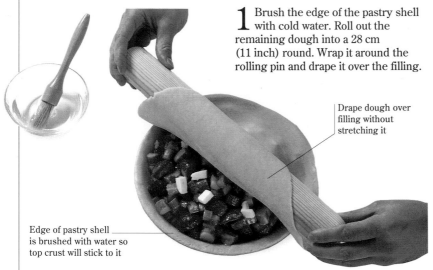

1 Brush the edge of the pastry shell with cold water. Roll out the remaining dough into a 28 cm (11 inch) round. Wrap it around the rolling pin and drape it over the filling.

Drape dough over filling without stretching it

Edge of pastry shell is brushed with water so top crust will stick to it

2 With the small knife, trim the top crust even with the bottom crust. Press the edges together to seal them.

3 Make a pastry rose with the dough trimmings (see box, below). Brush a little cold water onto the centre of the top crust and press the rose on top.

4 With the small knife, cut steam vents around the top crust of the pie.

HOW TO MAKE A PASTRY ROSE

A pastry rose is a traditional decoration for sweet and savoury pies with a top crust. Simple to make with dough trimmings, it gives an effective finish to a pie.

1 Roll out dough into a 7.5 x 30 cm (3 x 12 inch) rectangle, 5 mm (¼ inch) thick. Flour and cut into 4 squares. Stack.

2 Balance the squares on one forefinger. Pull the corners downwards and squeeze the layers in the other hand to make a ball.

3 With a small knife, and without cutting through to the base, cut a deep cross in the smooth upper surface of the ball of dough.

4 Open out the layers of dough to form the rose petals. Cut off and discard the dough from the base of the rose.

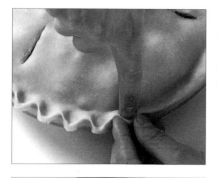

5 Scallop the edge of the pie: place the forefinger of one hand on the edge of the dough, pointing outwards. With the forefinger and thumb of your other hand, push dough inwards to form scallops. Repeat around the pie.

Skewer test is quick and easy

VARIATION
TRADITIONAL APPLE PIE
Serve this classic pie hot, with a slice of Cheddar cheese or a scoop of ice cream.

6 Brush the top crust with the milk, and sprinkle with the sugar. Chill until firm, about 15 minutes. Heat the oven to 220°C (425°F, Gas 7). Put the baking sheet in the oven to heat.

Golden pastry rose is pretty finishing touch

7 Bake the pie on the baking sheet in the oven, 20 minutes. Reduce the temperature to 180°C (350°F, Gas 4) and bake until the rhubarb is tender when pierced with the skewer through a steam vent, and the crust is browned, 30–35 minutes longer. Transfer to the wire rack, and let cool.

🍽 **TO SERVE**
Transfer the pie dish to a serving platter. Cut the pie into wedges and serve warm, or at room temperature.

1 Omit the rhubarb, strawberries, and orange. Make and chill the pie pastry dough, and line the pie dish as directed. Chill the shell as directed.
2 Peel 1 kg (2 lb) firm tart apples; then cut out the flower and stalk ends. Halve the apples and scoop out the cores. Set each apple half, cut-side down, on a chopping board and cut crosswise into medium slices. Transfer to a bowl. Sprinkle with the juice of 1 lemon.
3 Sprinkle 100 g (3 1/4 oz) sugar, 30 ml (2 tbsp) flour, 2.5 ml (1/2 tsp) ground cinnamon, 1.25 ml (1/4 tsp) ground nutmeg, and a pinch of salt over the apples. Toss until coated. Taste the apples, adding more sugar or spice, if you like.
4 Roll out the remaining dough and cover the pie as directed. With a small knife, cut an "x" in the centre of the top crust. Gently pull back the point of each triangle to reveal the filling. Scallop the edge as directed, but push inwards at an angle to make a sharper scallop.
5 Roll out the dough trimmings into a narrow 50 cm (20 inch) strip. Cut it lengthwise into two 3 mm (1/8 inch) strips. Brush the top crust with a little cold water and lay the strips in a wavy criss-cross pattern around it. Finish and bake the pie as directed. Serve hot.

LEMON TART

Tarte au Citron

¶◉¶ SERVES 8   ↩ WORK TIME 40–45 MINUTES*   ≋ BAKING TIME 25–30 MINUTES**

EQUIPMENT

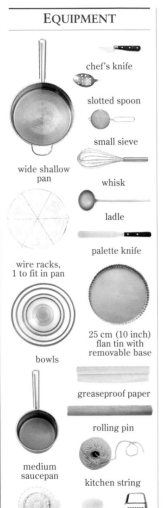

chef's knife

slotted spoon

small sieve

wide shallow pan

whisk

ladle

palette knife

wire racks, 1 to fit in pan

25 cm (10 inch) flan tin with removable base

bowls

greaseproof paper

rolling pin

medium saucepan

kitchen string

lemon squeezer

pastry scraper

grater

aluminium foil

kitchen scissors

baking sheet

rice

This recipe, with a filling of citrus zest and juice in a smooth custard, is the inspiration of Maurice Ferré from Maxim's restaurant in Paris.

GETTING AHEAD

Candy the lemon slices at least 1 day, and up to 2 days, ahead, and keep them at room temperature. The dough can be made up to 1 day ahead and kept, tightly wrapped, in the refrigerator. Bake the tart not more than 8 hours in advance, and add the candied lemon slices just before serving.

*plus 24 hours standing for candied lemon slices
and 45 minutes chilling for pâte sucrée dough
**plus 15 minutes baking blind

metric	SHOPPING LIST	imperial
1	orange	1
3	lemons	3
3	eggs	3
1	egg yolk	1
150 g	caster sugar	5 oz
	For the candied lemon slices	
2	lemons	2
250 g	caster sugar	8 oz
500 ml	water	16 fl oz
	For the pâte sucrée dough	
215 g	plain flour, more if needed	7 oz
90 g	unsalted butter, more for flan tin	3 oz
60 g	caster sugar	2 oz
2.5 ml	vanilla essence	½ tsp
1.25 ml	salt	¼ tsp
3	egg yolks	3

INGREDIENTS

lemons

orange

egg yolks

caster sugar

plain flour

eggs

vanilla essence

unsalted butter

ANNE SAYS

"The lemon slices must be candied at least 1 day ahead, so, if you are short of time, you can omit them and decorate the tart with rosettes of Chantilly cream."

ORDER OF WORK

1 CANDY THE LEMON SLICES

2 MAKE THE DOUGH, LINE THE FLAN TIN, AND BAKE THE PASTRY SHELL BLIND

3 MAKE THE FILLING; FILL AND FINISH THE TART

1 CANDY THE LEMON SLICES

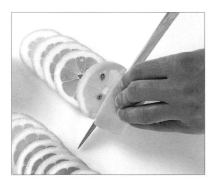

1 Trim off the ends from the lemons. Cut each lemon into 3 mm (¹⁄₈ inch) slices; discard any seeds.

2 Bring a medium saucepan of water to a boil. Add the lemon slices and simmer to blanch the slices just until they begin to soften, about 3 minutes. With the slotted spoon, remove a few lemon slices at a time. Let drain.

Lemon slices should be just covered with water

3 Attach three lengths of kitchen string to an upturned round wire rack. Heat the sugar and water in the wide shallow pan until dissolved, then bring just to a boil. Put the lemon slices on the rack, tie the strings together, and lower into the syrup. Press a round of greaseproof paper on top.

4 Bring the syrup slowly to a simmer, taking 10–12 minutes. Poach the lemon slices until tender to the bite, about 1 hour. Add more water during cooking, if necessary, so the slices are always covered. Take the pan from the heat and let the candied lemon slices cool in the syrup. Let stand in the syrup, covered with the paper round, at room temperature, 24 hours.

String handle makes lowering and lifting rack from pan easy

2 MAKE THE DOUGH, LINE THE FLAN TIN, AND BAKE THE PASTRY SHELL BLIND

1 Make and chill the dough (see box, page 18). Brush the tin with melted butter. Lightly flour the work surface; roll out the dough into a 30 cm (12 inch) round. Wrap it around the rolling pin and drape it over the tin.

2 Gently lift the edge of the dough with one hand, and press it into the bottom of the tin with the other hand. Overlap the dough slightly inside the tin rim. Roll the rolling pin over the top of the tin to cut off excess dough.

3 With your thumbs, press the dough evenly up the side of the flan tin, from the bottom edge, to increase the height of the pastry rim. Chill the pastry shell until it is firm, about 15 minutes.

4 Heat the oven to 200°C (400°F, Gas 6). Put the baking sheet in the oven. Line the shell with a double thickness of foil. Half-fill with rice.

5 Bake the shell on the baking sheet until set and the rim starts to brown, 10 minutes. Remove foil and rice. Reduce oven temperature to 190°C (375°F, Gas 5). Continue baking until pale brown, about 5 minutes longer. Leave the oven on. Transfer the shell in its tin to a wire rack. Let cool slightly.

3 MAKE THE FILLING; FILL AND FINISH THE TART

1 Grate the zest from the orange and lemons, then squeeze the fruit and strain the juice. There should be 250 ml (8 fl oz).

Orange juice mellows tartness of lemon juice

Coloured zest should be grated without any bitter white pith

2 Put the eggs, egg yolk, and sugar in a medium bowl. Add the orange and lemon zest and juice, and whisk together until thoroughly combined.

3 Set the pastry shell on the baking sheet Ladle the filling into the pastry shell, then bake in the heated oven until set, 25–30 minutes.

4 Transfer the tart to the wire rack and let cool slightly. Set the tart on a bowl to loosen and remove the side.

Side of flan tin slips off easily

5 Slide the tart from the tin base onto a flat platter and let cool to room temperature. Lift the rack of candied lemon slices out of the syrup and drain, 1–2 minutes.

6 Using the palette knife, arrange the candied lemon slices over the filling, starting at the edge. Serve, cut into wedges.

Candied lemon slices complete the tart

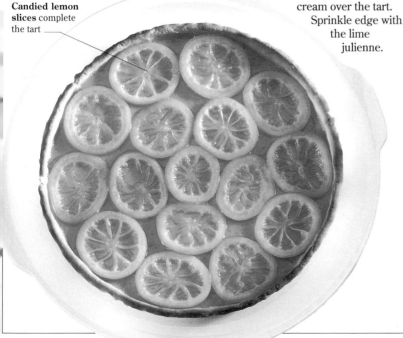

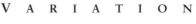

VARIATION
LIME AND CARDAMOM TART

This tart, with its smooth and creamy lime custard filling, is topped with piped Chantilly cream and lime julienne.

1 Substitute 4 limes for 4 of the lemons; omit the sugar and water for candying. Make and chill dough, line tin, and bake shell blind as directed.
2 Pare the zest from 1 lime. Cut into very fine julienne strips. Bring a small saucepan of water to a boil, add the zest strips, and simmer to blanch, 2–3 minutes. Drain, rinse in cold water, and drain again thoroughly.
3 Grate the zest from 2 of the remaining limes and from the lemon, then squeeze the juice from the lemon and all 4 limes; there should be 175 ml (6 fl oz) juice. Make the filling as directed, using the lime and lemon juice and zest, and adding 150 ml (1/4 pint) double cream, and 2.5 ml (1/2 tsp) ground cardamom. Bake, cool, and unmould the tart as directed.
4 Make the Chantilly cream (see box, right), using 250 ml (8 fl oz) double cream, 2.5 ml (1/2 tsp) vanilla essence, and 15 ml (1 tbsp) icing sugar. Put the cream into a piping bag fitted with a medium star nozzle; pipe cream over the tart. Sprinkle edge with the lime julienne.

HOW TO MAKE CHANTILLY CREAM

1 Pour double cream into a chilled bowl. Whip with a whisk or electric mixer until it forms soft peaks. Add flavouring and sugar; whip until the cream forms soft peaks again.

2 Continue whipping until the cream forms stiff peaks and the whisk leaves clear marks. Do not overwhip or cream will separate.

PEAR PIE WITH WALNUT PASTRY

Le Poirat

 SERVES 6–8   WORK TIME 35–40 MINUTES*   BAKING TIME 35–40 MINUTES

EQUIPMENT

23 cm (9 inch) flan tin with removable base

food processor †

sieve

chef's knife

small knife

vegetable peeler

pastry brush

pastry scraper

peppermill

6 cm (2½ inch) pastry cutter

bowls

wire rack

chopping board

baking sheet

rolling pin

lemon squeezer

metal skewer

† rotary cheese grater can also be used

In this speciality from central France, wedges of pear are sandwiched between a double crust of walnut pastry. Serve the pie warm, accompanied by crème fraîche or whipped double cream.

GETTING AHEAD

The walnut pastry dough can be made up to 2 days ahead and kept, tightly wrapped, in the refrigerator. The pie is best served the day of baking, but it can be stored in an airtight container, up to 1 day. Warm it in a low oven and add the crème fraîche just before serving.

*plus 2 ¼ hours chilling time

metric	SHOPPING LIST	imperial
1	lemon	1
875 g	pears	1¾ lb
2.5 ml	freshly ground black pepper	½ tsp
15 ml	caster sugar	1 tbsp
	crème fraîche (see box, page 44) for serving (optional)	
	For the walnut pastry dough	
60 g	walnut pieces	2 oz
135 g	caster sugar	4½ oz
250 g	plain flour, more if needed	9 oz
150 g	unsalted butter, more for flan tin	5 oz
1	egg	1
2.5 ml	salt	½ tsp
5 ml	ground cinnamon	1 tsp

INGREDIENTS

walnut pieces

pears

lemon

unsalted butter

caster sugar

ground cinnamon

black peppercorns

plain flour

egg

ANNE SAYS

"*Crème fraîche is easy but time-consuming to make. You can buy it at some supermarkets, or use whipped double cream instead.*"

ORDER OF WORK

1. MAKE THE WALNUT PASTRY DOUGH

2. ROLL OUT THE WALNUT PASTRY DOUGH AND LINE THE FLAN TIN

3. FILL, COVER, AND BAKE THE PIE

MAKE THE WALNUT PASTRY DOUGH

1 Put the walnut pieces in the food processor. Add about half of the sugar and finely grind. Alternatively, grind the walnuts in a rotary cheese grater, then mix with half of the sugar.

ANNE SAYS

"The sugar helps keep the walnuts from becoming oily in the food processor."

2 Sift the flour onto the work surface, add the ground walnut and sugar mixture, then make a large well in the centre of the ingredients. Using the rolling pin, pound the butter to soften it slightly.

3 Put the egg, the remaining sugar, the softened butter, salt, and ground cinnamon into the well. With your fingertips, work the ingredients in the well until they are all thoroughly mixed together.

Dough will be moist enough to come together easily when worked with your fingers

4 Draw in the flour with the pastry scraper, then work the flour into the other ingredients with your fingers until coarse crumbs form.

6 Sprinkle the work surface lightly with flour. Blend the dough by pushing it away from you with the heel of your hand. Gather up the dough and continue to blend in this manner until it is very smooth and peels away from the work surface in one piece, 1–2 minutes. Shape into a smooth ball, wrap tightly, and chill until firm, 1 hour.

Knead thoroughly to combine ingredients so dough is very pliable

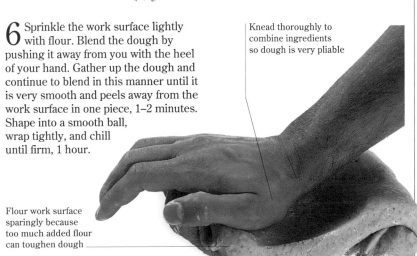

5 Press the dough gently into a ball. It should be quite soft, but if it is too sticky, add a little more flour.

Flour work surface sparingly because too much added flour can toughen dough

2 ROLL OUT THE WALNUT PASTRY DOUGH AND LINE THE FLAN TIN

1 Brush the flan tin with melted butter. Lightly flour the work surface. Roll out two-thirds of the chilled dough into a 28 cm (11 inch) round. Rewrap and return the unrolled dough to the refrigerator.

Apply even pressure to rolling pin

2 Wrap the dough around the rolling pin. Gently drape it over the tin.

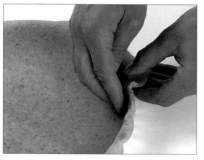

3 Lift edge of dough with one hand and press it into the bottom of the tin with the other hand. Overlap the dough slightly inside the rim of the tin, so extra dough is left at the edge.

4 Roll the rolling pin over the top of the tin, pressing down to cut off the excess dough. Add the trimmings to the reserved portion of dough and return to the refrigerator.

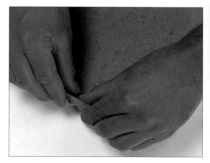

5 With your thumbs, press the dough evenly up the tin side to increase the height of the shell. Chill the shell until very firm, about 1 hour. Meanwhile, prepare the pears.

3 FILL, COVER, AND BAKE THE PIE

1 Squeeze the juice from the lemon. Peel the pears with the vegetable peeler, from stalk to flower ends.

Lemon juice will keep peeled and quartered pears from discolouring

2 Using the tip of the small knife, cut out the stalk and flower ends from each pear.

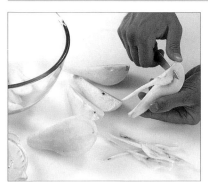

3 Cut each pear into quarters, then scoop out the central stalks and cores with the small knife.

4 Put the pear wedges into a medium bowl. Add the black pepper and the lemon juice. Toss until the pear wedges are coated.

5 Shaking off any excess lemon juice, arrange the pear wedges evenly in a cartwheel pattern on the bottom of the pastry shell.

Quartered pears fit neatly in pastry shell

6 Roll out the remaining dough into a 25 cm (10 inch) round; stamp out a 5 cm (2½ inch) round from the centre, using the cutter.

ANNE SAYS
"You can also use a glass to stamp out the round."

Lay pear wedges on their sides, stalk ends inwards

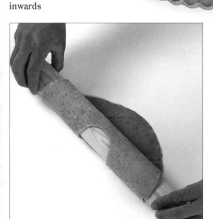

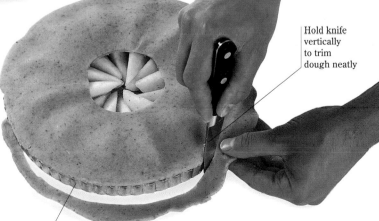

Hold knife vertically to trim dough neatly

7 Wrap the dough around the rolling pin and drape it carefully over the pear wedges.

Use flan tin as your guide to trim top crust

8 With the small knife, trim the top round even with the filled pastry shell, using the tin as a guide.

Apply gentle pressure with tines of fork

Dough settles around pear quarters and bakes in attractive petal pattern

9 Press the dough edges together with the back of a fork to seal the top and bottom of the pastry shell.

10 Brush the top with water and sprinkle with the sugar. Chill the pie until firm, about 15 minutes. Heat the oven to 190°C (375°F, Gas 5). Heat the baking sheet in the oven.

11 Put the chilled pear pie on the baking sheet and bake in the heated oven until the pastry is browned and the pears are tender when pierced with the metal skewer, 35–40 minutes.

CREME FRAICHE

When unpasteurized cream is left to stand, it develops a full, slightly sour taste. This is crème fraîche, the cream most frequently used in France. Modern production methods use recultured pasteurized cream. This recipe is my own homemade version of crème fraîche.

 MAKES 375 ML (12 FL OZ)

 WORK TIME 12–15 MINUTES

STANDING TIME 6–8 HOURS

SHOPPING LIST

250 ml	double cream	8 fl oz
125 ml	buttermilk, or soured cream plus 2.5 ml (½ tsp) lemon juice	4 fl oz

1 Pour the double cream into a saucepan and add the buttermilk. Alternatively, add the soured cream and lemon juice. Stir to mix. Heat gently until barely warm, 24°C (75°F). Pour the mixture into a glass bowl.

2 Cover, leaving a gap for air. Leave at room temperature, 21°C (70°F), until the cream has thickened enough to hold the mark of a spoon and tastes slightly acidic, 6–8 hours. Stir, cover, and chill.

12 Let the pie cool slightly, then, while it is still warm, set the flan tin on a bowl to loosen and remove the side. Slide the pie from the tin base onto a serving plate.

🍴 TO SERVE
Cut the warm pie into wedges and transfer to individual plates. Accompany each serving with a generous spoonful of crème fraîche, if using, and serve at once. Serve the remaining crème fraîche in a separate bowl.

Sweet walnut dough bakes brown and crisp

VARIATION
PEACH PIE WITH WALNUT PASTRY
When summer peaches are ripe, I like to bake them in this variation of Pear Pie with Walnut Pastry and serve the pie with ice cream.

1 Omit the pears and freshly ground black pepper. Make and chill the walnut pastry dough, line the flan tin, and chill the pastry shell as directed.
2 Scald, stone, and peel 750 g (1½ lb) peaches: bring a saucepan of water to a boil. Immerse the peaches in the water, 10 seconds, then transfer them with a slotted spoon to a bowl of cold water.

3 With a small knife, cut 1 peach in half, using the indentation on one side as a guide. Twist with both hands to loosen the peach halves from the stone, and pull them apart. If the peach clings, loosen the flesh from the stone with a small knife. Scoop out the stone with the tip of the knife and discard it. Repeat for the rest of the peaches. Peel the skin from the peach halves and cut each half into 2–3 wedges. Toss the peaches in the lemon juice.
4 Arrange the peaches in the pastry shell. Cover, bake, and finish the pie as directed.
5 Cut the warm pie into wedges and serve at once. Accompany with scoops of vanilla ice cream, served separately, if you like.

CHOCOLATE PYE WITH A CRUNCHY CRUST

🍴 SERVES 8   🥄 WORK TIME 30–35 MINUTES*   🍲 BAKING TIME 15–20 MINUTES**

EQUIPMENT

chef's knife

pastry brush

25 cm (10 inch) flan tin with removable base

bowls

food processor †

whisk

wooden spoon

rose leaves

wire rack

baking sheet

saucepans

rubber spatula

rolling pin

chopping board

†rotary cheese grater can also be used

A velvety combination of dark chocolate and cream fills a crisp almond crust. Although the pastry for this attractive "pye" dates back to eighteenth-century England, the decoration follows a modern style.

GETTING AHEAD

The crunchy crust can be made up to 1 day ahead and kept, tightly wrapped, in the refrigerator. The tart can be baked 1 day in advance. Keep it, covered, in the refrigerator and allow it to come to room temperature before serving.

*plus 45 minutes chilling
**plus 8–10 minutes baking blind

metric	SHOPPING LIST	imperial
270 g	plain chocolate	9 oz
375 ml	double cream	12 fl oz
2	eggs	2
1	egg yolk	1
	For the crunchy crust	
60 g	caster sugar	2 oz
175 g	blanched almonds	6 oz
1	egg white	1
	butter for flan tin	
	For the decoration	
90 g	white chocolate	3 oz

INGREDIENTS

plain chocolate

double cream

egg yolk

eggs

caster sugar

butter

blanched almonds

egg white

white chocolate

ORDER OF WORK

1 MAKE MIXTURE FOR THE CRUST

2 LINE THE TIN; BAKE THE CRUNCHY CRUST BLIND

3 MAKE THE FILLING AND DECORATION; FINISH THE TART

1 MAKE MIXTURE FOR THE CRUST

1 Put the sugar and blanched almonds in the food processor and finely grind them. Alternatively, grind just the almonds in a rotary cheese grater, then stir in the sugar.

ANNE SAYS
"The sugar helps keep the blanched almonds from becoming oily in the food processor."

2 In a medium bowl, whisk the egg white just until it is frothy.

3 Transfer the ground almond and sugar mixture from the food processor to the beaten egg white.

Mixture comes together easily with help of wooden spoon

4 Stir the mixture with the wooden spoon to form a stiff paste. Shape it into a ball, wrap tightly, and chill until firm, about 30 minutes.

2 LINE THE TIN; BAKE THE CRUNCHY CRUST BLIND

1 Melt a little butter in a small saucepan, then brush the flan tin with the melted butter.

Rolling pin is ideal for flattening mixture

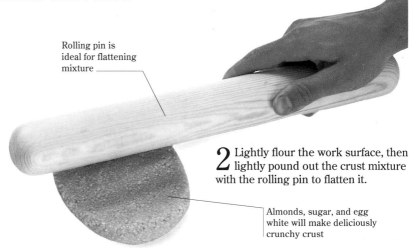

2 Lightly flour the work surface, then lightly pound out the crust mixture with the rolling pin to flatten it.

Almonds, sugar, and egg white will make deliciously crunchy crust

3 Transfer the crust mixture to the flan tin. With the back of a spoon, dipped into cold water, or with the heel of your hand, press the mixture into the bottom of the tin, then push it well up the side. Chill until firm, about 15 minutes.

Crust mixture is easy to spread when spoon is dipped into cold water

4 Heat the oven to 180°C (350°F, Gas 4). Put the baking sheet in the oven to heat. Put the shell on the baking sheet, and bake in the heated oven just until it is lightly browned, 8–10 minutes. Slide the shell off the baking sheet, onto the wire rack. Let the crunchy crust cool in the tin. Leave the oven on while you are making the chocolate filling for the tart.

HOW TO CHOP CHOCOLATE

If necessary, chill chocolate before chopping. Use a dry chopping board because moisture can affect melting. Work quickly to keep chocolate from melting on the board.

Rocking action makes it quick and easy to chop chocolate

1 Put the chocolate on a chopping board. With a chef's knife, cut the chocolate into small chunks.

2 To chop by hand:
With broad end of knife, chop until fine. Rock handle up and down, holding tip down with the heel of other hand.

To chop in a food processor:
Put the chocolate chunks into a food processor, then chop, using the pulse button. If necessary, chop the chunks in several batches.

! TAKE CARE !
Do not overwork the chocolate or the heat of the machine may melt it.

3 MAKE THE FILLING AND DECORATION; FINISH THE TART

1 Chop the plain chocolate (see box, page 48) and put it into a medium bowl. In a saucepan, bring the cream just to a boil. Pour the cream over the chocolate.

When chocolate melts in hot cream, mixture will darken in colour

2 Whisk the chocolate and cream together until the chocolate has melted completely. Set the mixture aside to cool to tepid.

3 Put the eggs and the egg yolk into another bowl, and whisk them together until mixed.

4 Whisk the tepid chocolate and cream mixture into the beaten eggs just to combine.

5 Carefully pour the filling into the cooled shell. Put the tart on the baking sheet, and bake in the oven until the filling begins to set, but is still soft in the centre, 15–20 minutes.

Filling is smooth and rich

6 Let the tart cool slightly on the wire rack, then carefully loosen the pastry from the side of the tin. Set the flan tin on a bowl and remove the side. Slide the tart from the tin base onto the wire rack to cool thoroughly.

ANNE SAYS
"Here, ganache, a mixture of boiled double cream and melted chocolate, is combined with eggs to make chocolate custard to fill the tart."

HOW TO MAKE CHOCOLATE LEAVES

White and plain chocolate facsimiles can be made of pliable leaves with deep veins, such as rose leaves. Chocolate leaves can be layered with greaseproof paper, then stored in the refrigerator, up to 1 week.

1 Put the chopped chocolate in a small bowl set over a saucepan half-filled with hot water. Heat very gently, stirring occasionally with a wooden spoon, just until the chocolate has melted, 2–3 minutes.

2 Spread the chocolate on the underside of each leaf in a thin, even layer, leaving a little of the stalk exposed. Drape some leaves on the handle of a wooden spoon so they curl; set the rest on a plate to keep them flat. Cool, then chill until set.

3 With the tips of your thumb and forefinger, peel away each rose leaf from the chocolate, handling as little as possible so the chocolate does not melt and become dull.

Moist chocolate filling is delicious set in crispy almond crust

7 Meanwhile, chop the white chocolate in the same way as the plain chocolate (see box, page 48), and use to make 15–20 chocolate leaves (see box, above). Transfer the tart to a serving plate and decorate with the chocolate leaves.

⊙️ TO SERVE
Serve the chocolate tart at room temperature, cut into wedges.

CHOCOLATE AND CHESTNUT PYE WITH A CRUNCHY CRUST

Mixed in this chocolate tart, chestnuts are a real treat. Sumptuous chocolate curls make the perfect finishing touch.

1 Make the crunchy crust mixture, line the flan tin, and bake the shell blind as directed in the main recipe.
2 Lightly crush 175 g (6 oz) peeled canned or vacuum-packed chestnuts. Sprinkle the crushed chestnuts evenly over the bottom of the shell.
3 Make the chocolate filling, pour it over the chestnuts, and bake the tart as directed. Let cool.
4 Omit the white chocolate decoration. Make long chocolate curls: melt 90 g (3 oz) plain chocolate as for the white chocolate. With a palette knife, spread the melted chocolate on a baking sheet in an even, thin layer. Leave until the chocolate has just set, 15–20 minutes. Holding a palette knife or a metal spatula at a 45° angle, push the blade away from you across the chocolate to form long curls.
5 Arrange the chocolate curls in a spoke pattern on top of the tart. Sift 15 ml (1 tbsp) cocoa powder over the chocolate curls.
6 Transfer the tart to a serving plate. Serve the tart at room temperature, cut into wedges.

CHOCOLATE MINT PYE WITH A CRUNCHY CRUST

Crushed fresh mint infuses the double cream to add a refreshing flavour to this version of Chocolate Pye with a Crunchy Crust. The white chocolate decoration is piped.

1 Make the crunchy crust mixture, line the flan tin, and bake the shell blind as directed in the main recipe.
2 Rinse 1 large bunch of fresh mint (about 90 g/3 oz). Reserve 8 small sprigs of mint for decoration. Put the remaining mint sprigs in a medium saucepan and lightly crush them, using the end of a rolling pin.
3 Pour the double cream over the crushed mint and bring just to a boil. Remove from the heat, cover, and set aside to infuse, 10–15 minutes.
4 Chop the plain chocolate as directed, and place in a bowl. Bring the cream just back to a boil, then pour it through a sieve into the bowl of chopped chocolate. Finish the filling and bake the tart as directed.

5 Snip off a corner from the bottom of a small plastic bag and use as a piping bag for piping the white chocolate decoration. Melt the white chocolate as directed and spoon it into the prepared plastic bag. Pipe the melted chocolate decoratively over the tart and leave until firm. Serve the tart at room temperature, cut into wedges, and decorate each serving with a reserved mint sprig.

STRAWBERRY MOUSSE PIE

🍽 SERVES 6–8   🥄 WORK TIME 40–45 MINUTES*   ❄ SETTING TIME 1–2 HOURS

EQUIPMENT

- electric mixer
- food processor †
- small knife
- pastry brush
- 23 cm (9 inch) pie dish
- saucepans, 1 heavy-based
- sieve
- whisk
- wire rack
- bowls
- rolling pin
- pastry scraper
- aluminium foil
- dried beans ‡
- chopping board
- baking sheet
- rubber spatula

† chef's knife can also be used
‡ rice can also be used

A cross between mousse and soufflé, the strawberry and cream filling in this pie is lightly set with a small amount of gelatine. Traditionally called Bavarian creams, mixtures like these are often used in charlottes and moulded desserts.

GETTING AHEAD

The dough can be made up to 2 days ahead and kept, tightly wrapped, in the refrigerator. Though best on the day of baking, when the mousse is fresh, the pie can be assembled up to 1 day ahead and kept, covered, in the refrigerator.

*plus 45 minutes chilling and 17–25 minutes baking blind

metric	SHOPPING LIST	imperial
500 g	strawberries	1 lb
250 ml	double cream	8 fl oz
10 ml	powdered gelatine	2 tsp
30 ml	water	2 tbsp
100 g	sugar	3 1/4 oz
2	egg yolks	2
8	sprigs of fresh mint	8
For the chocolate pastry dough		
150 g	plain flour, more if needed	5 oz
30 ml	cocoa powder	2 tbsp
90 g	unsalted butter, more for pie dish	3 oz
3	egg yolks	3
60 g	caster sugar	2 oz
1.25 ml	salt	1/4 tsp
2.5 ml	vanilla essence	1/2 tsp

INGREDIENTS

- strawberries
- double cream

- unsalted butter
- cocoa powder

- egg yolks
- plain flour

- powdered gelatine
- caster sugar
- fresh mint
- vanilla essence

ANNE SAYS

"The filling can be made with other fruit purées, but I like to use strawberries because the pale pink of the mousse offsets the dark chocolate crust."

ORDER OF WORK

1 MAKE THE CHOCOLATE PASTRY DOUGH

2 LINE THE DISH AND BAKE THE PASTRY SHELL BLIND

3 MAKE THE FILLING AND FINISH THE PIE

1 MAKE THE CHOCOLATE PASTRY DOUGH

1 Sift the flour and cocoa powder onto the work surface and make a large well in the centre.

Pound butter lightly, so it is softened but not sticky

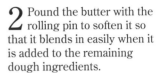

2 Pound the butter with the rolling pin to soften it so that it blends in easily when it is added to the remaining dough ingredients.

Cocoa gives colour as well as flavour to dough

3 Put the egg yolks, sugar, salt, vanilla essence, and softened butter into the well.

Softened butter will blend easily with ingredients in well

5 Gradually draw in the flour and cocoa powder with the pastry scraper, working them into the other ingredients with your fingertips.

4 Using your fingertips, work all the ingredients in the well together until thoroughly mixed.

Mix ingredients in well with fingertips of one hand

6 Continue working the ingredients with your fingertips until coarse crumbs form. Press the dough into a ball. If the dough is sticky, work in a little more flour.

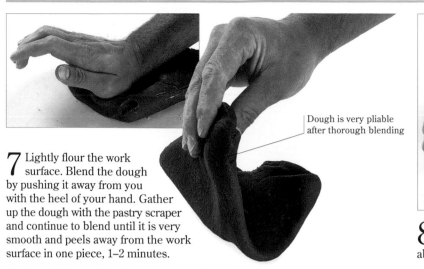

Dough is very pliable after thorough blending

7 Lightly flour the work surface. Blend the dough by pushing it away from you with the heel of your hand. Gather up the dough with the pastry scraper and continue to blend until it is very smooth and peels away from the work surface in one piece, 1–2 minutes.

8 Shape the dough into a ball again, wrap it tightly, and chill until firm, about 30 minutes.

2 LINE THE DISH AND BAKE THE PASTRY SHELL BLIND

1 Brush the pie dish with melted butter. Lightly flour the work surface, and roll out the chilled dough into a round 5 cm (2 inches) larger than the top of the pie dish. Wrap the dough around the rolling pin and drape it over the dish.

2 Gently lift the edge of the dough with the fingertips of one hand, and press it well into the bottom of the pie dish with the fingertips of the other hand, pressing lightly to seal any cracks.

Dough is easy to lift when wrapped around rolling pin

High dough edge is easy to scallop

3 Using a table knife, trim the pastry even with the outer edge of the dish. Pinch the dough to make the edge stand up. With one forefinger under the dough edge, pinch the top of the edge between your other forefinger and thumb to make a wide scallop.

Thumb and forefingers shape scallops easily

4 Prick the bottom of the pastry shell with a fork to prevent air bubbles forming during baking. Chill the shell until firm, about 15 minutes. Heat the oven to 200°C (400°F, Gas 6). Put the baking sheet in the oven to heat.

5 Line the shell with a double thickness of foil, pressing it well into the bottom edge. Half-fill the foil with dried beans to weigh down the dough. Bake on the baking sheet until the edge is set, 12–15 minutes.

6 Remove the foil and beans. Reduce the oven temperature to 180°C (350°F, Gas 4) and continue baking until the bottom of the pastry shell is firm, 5–10 minutes longer. Transfer the pastry shell to the wire rack to cool.

MAKE THE FILLING AND FINISH THE PIE

Strawberries are easy to hull with point of small sharp knife

Moist green hulls indicate freshness

1 Hull the strawberries, using the tip of the small knife. Wash them only if they are dirty. Set aside 8 of the strawberries for decoration.

2 In the food processor, work the strawberries to a coarse purée. Alternatively, chop the strawberries with the chef's knife.

3 Pour the cream into a chilled bowl, and whip with the electric mixer or a hand whisk until soft peaks form and the cream just holds its shape; cover and chill the cream.

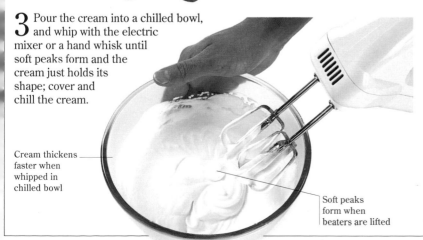

Cream thickens faster when whipped in chilled bowl

Soft peaks form when beaters are lifted

4 Sprinkle the gelatine evenly over the water in a small saucepan. Let soak, about 5 minutes. The gelatine will soften to a spongy consistency.

6 Heat the mixture, whisking constantly, just until it comes to a boil, 2–3 minutes; it will lighten and thicken slightly. Pour the mixture into a medium bowl. Let cool to tepid.

Whisk ingredients together thoroughly before mixture boils

5 In a medium heavy-based saucepan, combine the puréed strawberries, sugar, and egg yolks.

Mixture will start to set as soon as it is cold

7 Set the softened gelatine over low heat and melt it until pourable, shaking the saucepan occasionally, 1–2 minutes; do not stir the gelatine or it may become stringy.

8 Beat the tepid strawberry and egg yolk mixture with the electric mixer until light and frothy, 1–2 minutes. Pour the melted gelatine into the mixture and whisk until cool.

9 Set the bowl of strawberry filling in a larger bowl, half-filled with iced water, and stir gently until the mixture starts to thicken, 2–3 minutes. Remove the bowl from the bowl of iced water.

Stir mixture gently but constantly with rubber spatula so it thickens evenly

10 Add the chilled whipped cream and fold together gently, scooping under the mousse and then turning the mixture over. At the same time, turn the bowl anticlockwise.

VARIATION
COCONUT MOUSSE PIE

Fresh strawberries are replaced by a filling flavoured with toasted coconut and coconut milk. Canned coconut milk is available in most oriental food shops.

11 Pour the strawberry filling into the prepared pastry shell and chill until set, 1–2 hours. Just before serving, slice the reserved strawberries just to the stalk ends so they remain intact. Gently press each strawberry flat into a fan with your thumb.

TO SERVE
Arrange the fans on the set pie filling and place a mint sprig at each hull end. Transfer the pie dish to a serving platter. Cut the pie into wedges, using a knife dipped in hot water.

Dark chocolate crust forms frame around pale pink filling

1 Omit the strawberries. Make and chill the pastry dough, and line the pie dish as directed. Trim the edge of the dough even with the outer edge of the dish. With the tines of a table fork, mark lines around the edge of the pastry shell. Bake the pastry shell blind as directed. Leave the oven on.

2 Spread 90 g (3 oz) unsweetened shredded coconut on a baking tray and toast until golden brown, about 5 minutes. Stir occasionally so it browns evenly.

3 Whip the cream as directed.

4 Prepare the gelatine and make the filling as directed, adding 250 ml (8 fl oz) canned coconut milk to the egg yolks in place of the strawberry purée. Bring the mixture just to a boil, then let cool. If the mixture separates, whisk it to mix, then stir in half of the toasted coconut. Add the melted gelatine and the cream as directed.

5 Fill the pie as directed. Chill until the filling is set, 1–2 hours.

6 Coarsely grate 60 g (2 oz) plain chocolate. Sprinkle alternate bands of grated chocolate and the remaining toasted coconut crosswise over the pie and cut it into wedges for serving.

AMELIA SIMMONS' PUMPKIN PIE

EQUIPMENT

chef's knife

small knife

23 cm (9 inch) pie dish

pastry brush

palette knife

food processor

bowls

rolling pin

slotted spoon

colander

large pan, with lid

wire rack

aluminium foil

electric mixer

baking sheet

dried beans

sieve

scissors

rubber spatula

metal skewer

The first American cookbook, written by Amelia Simmons in 1796, included a pumpkin pie similar to this one. She suggested sweetening the filling with economical blackstrap molasses, but I use black treacle and a generous amount of sugar because they are more to our modern taste.

GETTING AHEAD

The dough can be made and the pumpkin can be cooked up to 2 days ahead. Keep them both, tightly wrapped, in the refrigerator. The pie is best eaten on the day of baking.

*plus 45 minutes chilling
**plus 15 minutes baking blind*

metric	SHOPPING LIST	imperial
1.15–1.4 kg	piece of pumpkin	2 1/2–3 lb
2	eggs	2
175 ml	double cream	6 fl oz
50 g	caster sugar	1 3/4 oz
2.5 ml	ground ginger	1/2 tsp
2.5 ml	ground nutmeg	1/2 tsp
1.25 ml	ground mace	1/4 tsp
60 ml	black treacle	2 fl oz
For the shortcrust pastry dough		
215 g	plain flour	7 oz
1.25 ml	salt	1/4 tsp
22.5 ml	caster sugar (optional)	1 1/2 tbsp
45 g	white vegetable shortening	1 1/2 oz
60 g	unsalted butter, more for pie dish	2 oz
45–60 ml	cold water, more if needed	3–4 tbsp

INGREDIENTS

black treacle

pumpkin †

caster sugar

vegetable shortening

plain flour

double cream

ground nutmeg

eggs

ground ginger

unsalted butter

ground mace

†375 ml (12 fl oz) canned pumpkin purée can also be used

ORDER OF WORK

1 MAKE THE SHORTCRUST PASTRY DOUGH; COOK AND PUREE THE PUMPKIN

2 LINE THE PIE DISH; MAKE THE DECORATION; BAKE SHELL BLIND

3 PREPARE THE FILLING AND BAKE THE PIE

1 MAKE THE SHORTCRUST PASTRY DOUGH; COOK AND PUREE THE PUMPKIN

1 Make the shortcrust pastry dough (see box, page 60). While the dough is chilling, prepare the pumpkin. Scoop out the seeds and pull out the fibrous threads from the pumpkin; discard them.

ANNE SAYS
"A large metal spoon is the best tool for removing pumpkin seeds."

Flesh of small pumpkins tends to be more succulent than flesh of large pumpkins

Seeds detach easily when pumpkin is ripe

2 Cut the pumpkin skin and flesh lengthwise into wedges, then crosswise into large chunks; put into the large pan. Pour in enough water to come one-quarter of the way up the pumpkin, cover, and simmer until the flesh is tender, 25–30 minutes.

When cooked, pumpkin flesh can be scraped easily from skin

3 With the slotted spoon, transfer the pumpkin to the colander and discard the cooking water.

4 With a metal spoon, scrape the pumpkin flesh into a bowl and discard the skin.

5 Transfer the pumpkin flesh to the food processor and purée until smooth. Alternatively, purée the flesh in batches in a blender.

6 Work the pumpkin purée through the sieve to remove any fibres. There should be about 375 ml (12 fl oz) pumpkin purée.

HOW TO MAKE SHORTCRUST PASTRY DOUGH IN A FOOD PROCESSOR

Shortcrust pastry dough can be made in a food processor fitted with a metal blade. Water is added gradually, while the blades are turning. Sugar is an optional ingredient.

1 Put the flour into a food processor. Add the salt, and sugar if using, and blend, about 5 seconds.

2 Cut the shortening and butter into small pieces and add the pieces to the flour mixture.

3 Work the mixture, using the pulse button, until it resembles coarse crumbs, 10–15 seconds.

4 Sprinkle the cold water over the mixture, 15 ml (1 tbsp) at a time, and work, using the pulse button, just until the crumbs start sticking together, 10–15 seconds. If the crumbs are dry and do not stick, add 15–30 ml (1–2 tbsp) water.

! TAKE CARE !
If too much water is added, the dough will be sticky and the pastry will be tough.

As water is mixed in, crumbs become larger and dough begins to hold together

5 Transfer the dough to the work surface and press lightly into a ball. Wrap the dough tightly and chill until firm, about 30 minutes.

2 LINE THE PIE DISH; MAKE THE DECORATION; BAKE SHELL BLIND

1 With the pastry brush, brush the pie dish with melted butter. Lightly flour the work surface and roll out the chilled dough into a round 5 cm (2 inches) larger than the top of the dish.

2 Wrap the dough around the rolling pin and drape it over the dish.

Dough hangs over edge of pie dish

3 Gently lift the edge of the dough with one hand and press it well into the bottom of the dish with the other hand, pressing gently to seal any cracks.

! TAKE CARE !
Be careful not to stretch the dough or it will shrink when baked.

After chilling, dough is pliable and easy to mould

Excess dough will be trimmed and reserved to make maple-leaf decoration

4 Using a table knife, trim off excess dough even with the outer edge of the dish and chill the trimmings. Pinch the dough edge between thumb and forefinger to make it stand up.

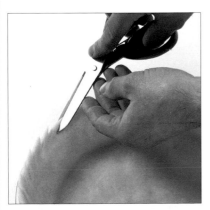

5 Feather the edge of the pastry shell: with the scissors, make 1.25 cm (½ inch) diagonal incisions around the rim at 1.25 cm (½ inch) intervals.

6 With your fingertips, push one point towards the centre of the shell, and the next point towards the edge. Continue around the edge. Prick the bottom of the shell with a fork. Chill until firm, about 15 minutes. Heat the oven to 200°C (400°F, Gas 6). Put the baking sheet in the oven to heat.

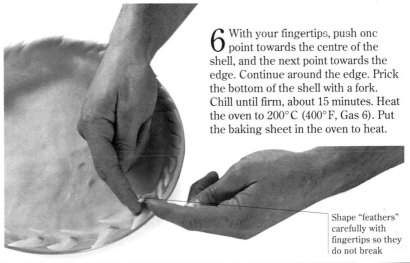

Shape "feathers" carefully with fingertips so they do not break

7 Meanwhile, roll out the dough trimmings and cut out 3 maple-leaf shapes about 7.5 cm (3 inches) across, using an illustration of a maple leaf as a guide, if necessary. Mark veins on the leaves with the back of the small knife; set the leaves on a plate and chill.

Veins on leaves have been marked by back of knife to avoid cutting dough

8 Line the prepared pastry shell with a double thickness of foil, pressing it well into the bottom edge. Half-fill the foil with dried beans or rice to weigh down the dough.

9 Bake the shell on the baking sheet in the heated oven until set and the shell rim just starts to brown, about 10 minutes. Remove the foil and beans or rice. Reduce the oven temperature to 180°C (350°F, Gas 4). Continue baking until lightly browned, about 5 minutes longer.

10 Transfer the pastry shell to the wire rack and let cool slightly.

PREPARE THE FILLING AND BAKE THE PIE

2 Beat the mixture with the electric mixer until thoroughly mixed. Alternatively, beat the mixture with a hand whisk.

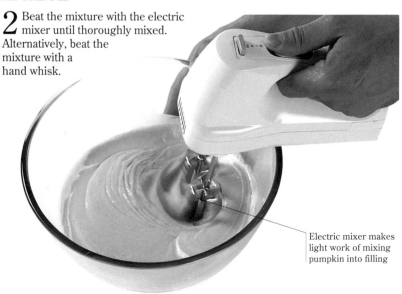

Electric mixer makes light work of mixing pumpkin into filling

1 Beat the eggs lightly until mixed. Add the cream and beaten eggs to the pumpkin purée.

3 Add the sugar, ground ginger, nutmeg, and mace. Pour in the treacle, and beat to combine.

4 Pour the pumpkin mixture into the shell and bake on the baking sheet in the heated oven, 20 minutes.

5 Add the leaves to the baking sheet and continue baking the pie, with the leaves, until the filling is firm and the metal skewer inserted in the centre comes out clean, 25–30 minutes longer. Transfer the pumpkin pie and the maple leaves to the wire rack and let cool.

¶◎¶ TO SERVE
Set the maple leaves on the filling, then transfer the pie dish to a serving platter. Cut the pie into wedges and serve from the dish at room temperature, with lightly whipped cream, if you like.

Treacle gives a gleaming dark finish to pumpkin pie

Maple leaves suggest autumn

PUMPKIN CRUNCH PIE

In this version, a pecan-crunch topping is sprinkled over the filling during baking.

1 Omit ground ginger and mace. Cook and purée the pumpkin as directed.
2 Make and chill the dough, and bake the pastry shell blind as directed.
3 Make the filling, adding 2.5 ml (1/2 tsp) each ground nutmeg and cinnamon, 1.25 ml (1/4 tsp) ground allspice, and a pinch of ground cloves.
4 Make the topping: coarsely chop 60 g (2 oz) pecans. Sift 30 g (1 oz) flour into a medium bowl. Stir in 60 g (2 oz) rolled oats. Add 45 ml (3 tbsp) unsalted butter and cut it into small pieces with a pastry blender or with 2 round-bladed knives. Rub with your fingertips until coarse crumbs form. Stir in 100 g (3 1/4 oz) brown sugar and the pecans.
5 Pour the filling into the pastry shell and bake in the heated oven, 15 minutes.
6 Sprinkle the topping evenly over the filling, and continue baking the pie until the filling is firm and the topping is crunchy and brown, 30–40 minutes longer.
7 Cut the pie into wedges and serve with lightly whipped cream, if you like.

ALMOND AND RASPBERRY TART

Linzertorte

 SERVES 6–8   WORK TIME 30–35 MINUTES*   BAKING TIME 40–45 MINUTES

EQUIPMENT

23 cm (9 inch) flan tin with removable base

sieves

 pastry brush

 lemon squeezer

 pastry scraper

palette knife

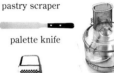 grater

food processor †

 wire rack

 bowls

 baking sheet

medium saucepan

fluted pastry wheel

rolling pin

wooden spoon

greaseproof paper

† rotary cheese grater can also be used

Now a Viennese speciality, this tart of buttery almond pastry and raspberry filling probably originated in the town of Linz in Austria. A lattice of pastry and a dusting of icing sugar decorate the tart.

GETTING AHEAD

The tart mellows if it is baked 1–2 days ahead and stored in an airtight container. Sprinkle it with icing sugar about 30 minutes before serving.

plus 1 1/4–2 1/4 hours chilling time

INGREDIENTS

 whole blanched almonds

 raspberries

 plain flour

 unsalted butter

 caster sugar

 egg yolk

 lemon

 icing sugar

 ground cinnamon

ground cloves

metric	SHOPPING LIST	imperial
375 g	raspberries	12 oz
125 g	caster sugar	4 oz
15–30 ml	icing sugar	1–2 tbsp
For the almond pastry dough		
1	lemon	1
175 g	whole blanched almonds	6 oz
125 g	plain flour, more if needed	4 oz
2.5 ml	ground cinnamon	1/2 tsp
1	pinch of ground cloves	1
125 g	unsalted butter, more for flan tin	4 oz
1	egg yolk	1
100 g	caster sugar	3 1/4 oz
1.25 ml	salt	1/4 tsp

ORDER OF WORK

1 MAKE THE ALMOND PASTRY DOUGH; MAKE THE RASPBERRY FILLING

2 LINE THE FLAN TIN AND FINISH THE TART

1 MAKE THE ALMOND PASTRY DOUGH; MAKE THE RASPBERRY FILLING

1 Grate the zest from the lemon onto a piece of greaseproof paper. Halve the lemon and squeeze about 22.5 ml (1½ tbsp) juice.

2 Put the whole almonds in the food processor, add half of the flour to prevent the almonds from becoming oily, and finely grind. Alternatively, grind the almonds by themselves in a rotary cheese grater.

3 Sift the remaining flour onto the work surface, with the cinnamon and cloves. Mix in the nuts, then make a well. Pound the butter to soften it. Put the butter, egg yolk, sugar, salt, lemon juice, and zest into the well.

4 Using your fingertips, work the ingredients in the well until thoroughly mixed. Draw in the flour and work it into the other ingredients until coarse crumbs form.

5 Press the dough into a ball, adding a little more flour if it is sticky. Lightly flour the work surface.

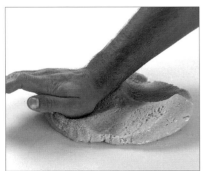

6 Blend the dough by pushing it away from you with the heel of your hand. Then gather it up with the pastry scraper and continue to blend until it is very smooth and peels away from the work surface in one piece, 1–2 minutes. Shape into a ball, wrap tightly, and chill until firm, 1–2 hours. While it is chilling, make the filling.

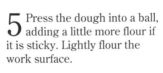

Break up raspberries with spoon

7 Pick over the raspberries; wash them only if dirty. Put the sugar and raspberries in the saucepan. Cook, stirring, until they form a thick pulpy jam, 10–12 minutes. Set aside to cool.

8 With the back of the wooden spoon, press half of the fruit pulp through a sieve, set over a bowl, to remove the seeds. Stir in the remaining pulp, leaving in seeds for texture.

2 LINE THE FLAN TIN AND FINISH THE TART

1 Brush the flan tin with melted butter. Lightly flour the work surface; roll out two-thirds of the dough into a 28 cm (11 inch) round. Rewrap and chill the remaining dough.

2 Wrap the dough around the rolling pin, then drape it over the tin. Lift the edge of the dough with one hand and press it into the bottom of the tin with the other hand. Overlap the dough slightly inside the tin rim.

3 Roll the rolling pin over the top of the tin to cut off the excess dough. Reserve the trimmings. With your thumbs, press the dough evenly up the side of the flan tin to increase the height of the shell.

4 Spread filling in shell. Roll out the remaining dough; trim to a 15 x 30 cm (6 x 12 inch) rectangle. Reserve the trimmings. Cut the dough into twelve 1.25 cm (1/2 inch) strips with the pastry wheel.

Fluted pastry wheel is simple to use

5 Carefully arrange half of the strips from left to right across the tart, about 2 cm (3/4 inch) apart. Turn the tart 45° and arrange the remaining strips diagonally over the first strips to form a lattice. Flour the rolling pin and roll it over the edge of the tin to trim the overhanging dough strips.

Palette knife makes it easy to lift fragile strips of dough

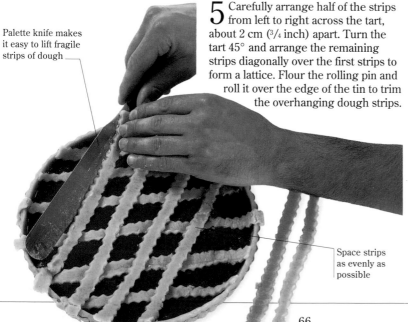

Space strips as evenly as possible

6 Roll all the dough trimmings into a long cylinder, then roll out thinly. Using the fluted pastry wheel, cut three to four 1.25 cm (1/2 inch) strips to go around the edge of the tart. Brush the edge of the tart with cold water. Arrange the strips around the edge, pressing with your fingertips. Chill until firm, about 15 minutes.

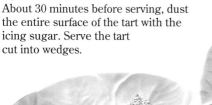

7 Heat the oven to 190°C (375°F, Gas 5). Put the baking sheet in the oven to heat. Bake the tart on the baking sheet until the pastry begins to brown, 15 minutes. Reduce the oven temperature to 180°C (350°F, Gas 4) and continue baking until the tart is golden brown and just beginning to shrink from the side of the flan tin, 25–30 minutes longer.

8 Transfer the tart to the wire rack and let cool slightly. Set the flan tin on a bowl to loosen and remove the side. Slide the tart from the tin base onto the wire rack and let cool completely.

Bowl gives firm support to flan tin

¶©¶ TO SERVE
About 30 minutes before serving, dust the entire surface of the tart with the icing sugar. Serve the tart cut into wedges.

HAZELNUT AND APRICOT TART
Curved strips of hazelnut pastry top an apricot filling baked in a hazelnut pastry shell.

1 Omit the raspberries. Substitute hazelnuts for the almonds. Spread on a baking sheet and toast in a 180°C (350°F, Gas 4) oven until browned, 10–12 minutes. Rub them in a tea towel to remove the skins; let cool. Make the dough and line the tin as directed.

2 Coarsely chop 375 g (12 oz) stoned dried apricots. In a pan, combine the apricots, 30–45 ml (2–3 tbsp) sugar, and water to cover. Simmer until reduced to a pulpy jam, 8–10 minutes. Let cool.

3 Spread the filling over the bottom of the shell. Roll out two-thirds of the remaining dough into a 6 x 30 cm (2½ x 12 inch) strip. With a fluted pastry wheel, cut lengthwise into 6 strips. Cut the strips in half. Set the end of 1 strip in the centre of the tart, curve it, and attach the other end to the outer edge. Continue, spacing the strips evenly around the tart. Trim the ends. Roll out the remaining dough, cut strips, and arrange around the edge of the tart as directed. Roll out the dough trimmings, cut into flower shapes, and set in the centre of the tart.

4 Chill, bake, and serve as directed.

PLAITED THREE-NUT PIE

🍽 SERVES 6–8   🥣 WORK TIME 35–40 MINUTES*   ♨ BAKING TIME 45–50 MINUTES**

EQUIPMENT

- 20 cm (8 inch) square cake tin†
- chef's knife
- whisk
- pastry brush
- small knife
- bowls
- rice‡
- wooden spoon
- rolling pin
- small saucepan
- aluminium foil
- tea towel
- baking sheet
- rubber spatula
- chopping board
- sieve
- metal skewer

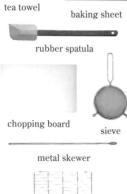

- wire racks

† 23 cm (9 inch) round pie dish can also be used
‡ dried beans can also be used

Inspired by the traditional American pecan pie, this pie combines walnuts, hazelnuts, and almonds in a light filling, decorated with plaits of pastry. Choose your own combination of nuts, or select your favourite nut. I like to bake this pie in a square cake tin for an unusual presentation.

GETTING AHEAD

The pie pastry dough can be made up to 2 days ahead and kept, tightly wrapped, in the refrigerator. The pie can be baked up to 1 day ahead and stored in an airtight container.

*plus 45 minutes chilling
**plus 15 minutes baking blind

metric	SHOPPING LIST	imperial
60 g	walnut halves	2 oz
60 g	whole blanched almonds	2 oz
30 g	hazelnuts	1 oz
60 g	unsalted butter, more for cake tin	2 oz
4	eggs	4
300 g	light soft brown sugar	10 oz
5 ml	vanilla essence	1 tsp
1.25 ml	salt	¼ tsp
15 ml	milk, for glaze	1 tbsp
	For the pie pastry dough	
330 g	plain flour	11 oz
2.5 ml	salt	½ tsp
150 g	white vegetable shortening	5 oz
90–100 ml	cold water, more if needed	6–7 tbsp

INGREDIENTS

 hazelnuts
 walnut halves
 whole blanched almonds
 eggs
 plain flour
 vanilla essence
 unsalted butter
 soft brown sugar
 milk
 vegetable shortening

ORDER OF WORK

1 MAKE THE PIE PASTRY DOUGH, LINE THE TIN, AND BAKE THE SHELL BLIND

2 PREPARE THE NUT FILLING AND FILL THE PASTRY SHELL

3 PLAIT AND BAKE THE PIE

1 MAKE THE PIE PASTRY DOUGH, LINE THE TIN, AND BAKE THE SHELL BLIND

1 Make the pie pastry dough (see box, below). Brush the cake tin with melted butter. Lightly flour the work surface. Roll out two-thirds of the dough and trim it to a 25 cm (10 inch) square. Return the remaining dough to the refrigerator.

2 Wrap the dough around the rolling pin and drape it over the cake tin.

Use rolling pin to lift dough so it does not tear

HOW TO MAKE PIE PASTRY DOUGH

Made with shortening, pie pastry is one of the quickest, easiest, and most versatile of doughs. It can be made even faster in a food processor, using the method given for Shortcrust Pastry Dough (see box, page 60). For a sweeter pastry, add 15–30 ml (1–2 tbsp) caster sugar with the flour.

1 Sift the flour and salt into a bowl. Add the shortening to the bowl.

Tap sieve to speed up sifting

2 Cut the shortening into the flour mixture with 2 round-bladed table knives or a pastry blender.

3 With your fingertips, rub the shortening into the flour until the mixture forms coarse crumbs, lifting and crumbling the mixture to help aerate it.

4 Sprinkle the water over the mixture, 15 ml (1 tbsp) at a time, and mix lightly with a fork.

5 When the crumbs are moist enough to start sticking together, press the dough lightly into a ball, wrap it tightly, and chill until firm, about 30 minutes.

Handle dough lightly or it will become elastic and hard to roll

3 Lift the edge of the dough with the fingertips of one hand, and press well into the bottom edges and up the sides of the tin with the fingertips of the other hand.

ANNE SAYS
"The height of tin sides varies, but the dough need not reach the rim when pressed up the tin sides."

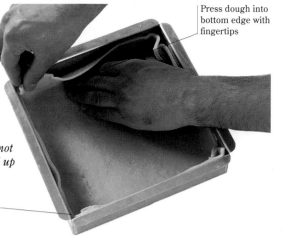

Press dough into bottom edge with fingertips

Seams of dough are pressed neatly into corners

4 Using a round-bladed table knife, trim the dough inside the tin, so that the shell is 4 cm (1½ inches) deep.

5 Prick the bottom of the pastry shell with a fork to prevent air bubbles forming during cooking. Chill until firm, about 15 minutes. Press the dough trimmings into the remaining dough, and chill. Heat the oven to 200°C (400°F, Gas 6). Put the baking sheet in the oven to heat.

6 Line the shell with a double thickness of foil, pressing it well into the corners. Half-fill the foil with rice. Bake the shell on the baking sheet in the heated oven until set, about 10 minutes.

7 Remove the foil and rice and continue baking, about 5 minutes longer.

Once dough is set, lining of foil filled with rice is removed so pastry can dry in oven

8 Let the shell cool slightly in the tin on the wire rack. Reduce the oven temperature to 180°C (350°F, Gas 4).

2 PREPARE THE NUT FILLING AND FILL THE PASTRY SHELL

1 Set aside one-third of the walnuts and almonds for decoration. Spread the remainder on the baking sheet and toast in the oven, stirring occasionally, until lightly browned, 8–10 minutes. Remove the nuts from the baking sheet.

Leave nuts quite coarse to add texture

Toasting develops flavour of nuts

2 Toast the hazelnuts as for the walnuts and almonds, allowing 12–15 minutes. Leave the oven on. While the hazelnuts are still hot, rub them in a rough tea towel to remove the skins. Let cool.

3 With the chef's knife, roughly chop the toasted walnuts, almonds, and hazelnuts. Melt the butter in the small saucepan. Let cool.

4 Put the eggs into a medium bowl. Add the brown sugar, and stir the eggs and sugar together with the whisk until they are evenly mixed.

Stir ingredients gently with whisk

5 Add the vanilla essence, salt, and cooled melted butter to the egg mixture, and stir until well combined.

Eggs and sugar form basis of filling

6 Add the toasted chopped walnuts, almonds, and hazelnuts to the filling mixture.

Rubber spatula
scrapes out
mixture

7 With the wooden spoon, stir the nuts into the filling mixture to distribute them evenly.

8 Carefully pour the filling into the pastry shell. Set the filled shell aside while making the pastry plaits.

3 PLAIT AND BAKE THE PIE

Plait strips carefully so they do not stretch or tear

1 Lightly flour the work surface. Roll out the remaining dough and trim to a 20 cm (8 inch) square. Cut it into 4 pieces. Leaving the dough attached at the top, cut each piece into 3 strips.

2 Plait 3 strips together, lifting them carefully over each other so they lie flat. Pinch the ends together, trim evenly, and put the braid on a plate. Repeat with the remaining strips to make 4 plaits. Chill.

ANNE SAYS
"Chilling the plaits helps them keep their shape while baking."

3 Meanwhile, bake the pie on the baking sheet in the heated oven just until it starts to set, 8–10 minutes. Lay the plaits along the edges of the filling and brush them with the milk to glaze. Arrange the reserved nuts decoratively on top of the filling.

4 Continue baking until the metal skewer inserted in the centre of the pie comes out clean, 35–40 minutes longer.

Pie must be cool before unmoulding or it will crumble

Hold tin and wire rack together firmly

5 Transfer the pie to a wire rack. Let cool to room temperature. When cool, transfer the wire rack to the top of the tin, turn both over together, then carefully lift off the tin. Set a second rack on the pie base and turn both over so the pie is right-side up. Slide the pie onto a serving platter.

🍴 **TO SERVE**
Serve the pie at room temperature. Cut into squares and transfer to individual plates.

Pastry plaits make unusual finish

Whole nuts decorate the serving platter

V A R I A T I O N

CLASSIC PECAN PIE

In this American favourite, walnuts, almonds, and hazelnuts are omitted, and only pecans are used. The sweet nut filling invites a simple accompaniment of fresh double cream. The edge of the pastry shell is scalloped with a dessert spoon – a simple method that creates a striking effect.

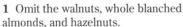

1 Omit the walnuts, whole blanched almonds, and hazelnuts.
2 Make the pie pastry dough as directed in the box on page 69, using 215 g (7 oz) flour, 125 g (4 oz) white vegetable shortening, 1.25 ml (¼ tsp) salt, and 45–60 ml (3–4 tbsp) cold water, more if needed.
3 Chill the dough as directed, about 30 minutes.

4 Brush a 23 cm (9 inch) pie dish with melted butter. Roll out the dough into a round 5 cm (2 inches) larger than the top of the pie dish. Wrap the dough around the rolling pin, then drape it over the dish. Gently lift the edge of the dough, then press it well into the bottom edge of the pie dish. Using a round-bladed knife, trim the excess dough even with the edge of the dish.

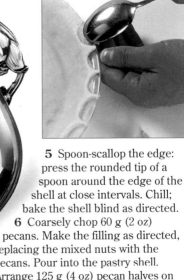

5 Spoon-scallop the edge: press the rounded tip of a spoon around the edge of the shell at close intervals. Chill; bake the shell blind as directed.
6 Coarsely chop 60 g (2 oz) pecans. Make the filling as directed, replacing the mixed nuts with the pecans. Pour into the pastry shell. Arrange 125 g (4 oz) pecan halves on top. Bake on the baking sheet in the 180°C (350°F, Gas 4) oven, 40–45 minutes. Serve from the dish, at room temperature, cut into wedges.

CARAMELIZED UPSIDE-DOWN MANGO TARTLETS

Tartelettes Tatin aux Mangues

 SERVES 6 WORK TIME 40–45 MINUTES* ♨ BAKING TIME 20–25 MINUTES

EQUIPMENT

chef's knife
palette knife
small knife
food processor †

six 10 cm (4 inch)
baking dishes ‡

bowls
tea towel

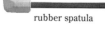
heavy-based saucepan
baking sheet

rolling pin

rubber spatula

chopping board

† blender can also be used

‡ six 10 cm (4 inch) tartlet tins with solid bases can also be used

The fame of Tarte Tatin, *with its apples and golden caramel, has spread worldwide, but I'm equally fond of this contemporary version, using mangoes. The tartlets are turned out to serve upside-down, and are best warm with chilled mango coulis.*

GETTING AHEAD

The dough can be made up to 2 days ahead and kept, tightly wrapped, in the refrigerator. The tartlets can be baked, and the coulis made up to 8 hours ahead. Refrigerate the coulis, and leave the tartlets in the dishes. To serve, warm in a 180°C (350°F, Gas 4) oven, about 10 minutes, then turn out.

plus 45 minutes chilling time

metric	SHOPPING LIST	imperial
200 g	caster sugar	6½ oz
125 ml	water	4 fl oz
4	medium mangoes, total weight about 1.5 kg (2½ lb)	4
	juice of ½ lime	
15–30 ml	icing sugar (optional)	1–2 tbsp
	For the pâte sucrée dough	
90 g	unsalted butter	3 oz
3	egg yolks	3
2.5 ml	vanilla essence	½ tsp
215 g	plain flour, more if needed	7 oz
60 g	caster sugar	2 oz
1.25 ml	salt	¼ tsp

INGREDIENTS

mangoes   unsalted butter   vanilla essence

lime juice   caster sugar

plain flour   egg yolks

ANNE SAYS

"Use mangoes that are ripe but still firm, so they do not produce too much juice during cooking."

ORDER OF WORK

1 MAKE THE DOUGH AND CARAMEL SYRUP

2 PREPARE THE MANGOES; FILL AND BAKE THE TARTLETS

3 MAKE THE MANGO COULIS; UNMOULD THE TARTLETS

1 MAKE THE DOUGH AND CARAMEL SYRUP

1 Make and chill the pâte sucrée dough (see box, page 76). Make the caramel syrup: put the sugar and water in the saucepan, and heat gently until dissolved, stirring occasionally. Boil, without stirring, until the mixture starts to turn golden around the edge.

Bubbles start to break more slowly and syrup turns golden

Boil sugar syrup briskly so water evaporates rapidly

! TAKE CARE !
Do not stir the sugar syrup during boiling or it may crystallize.

2 Lower the heat and continue cooking, swirling the saucepan once or twice so the syrup colours evenly, until the caramel is golden.

! TAKE CARE !
Cook the caramel only until medium gold; if too dark it will become bitter when it cooks further in the oven.

3 Remove the saucepan from the heat and immediately plunge the base of the saucepan into a bowl of cold water until cooking stops.

4 Pour about one-sixth of the caramel into the bottom of a baking dish. Working quickly, tilt the dish so the bottom is coated with a thin, even layer. Repeat with the remaining dishes. Let cool.

Tip and rotate dish to spread caramel evenly

2 PREPARE THE MANGOES; FILL AND BAKE THE TARTLETS

2 Cut each mango lengthwise on both sides of the stone so the knife just misses the stone. Cut the remaining mango flesh away from each stone in 2 long slices and set aside for the coulis. Discard the stones.

Trim as close to stone as possible

1 Peel each of the mangoes with the small knife, taking care to remove the minimum amount of mango flesh with the skin.

3 Cut each of the large pieces of mango into 3 diagonal slices. Arrange 3 slices, cut-side up, on top of the caramel in one dish. Repeat until all the dishes are filled. Add the remaining slices to the mango for the coulis.

4 Lightly flour the work surface. With your hands, shape the dough into a cylinder about 30 cm (12 inches) long. Cut it into 6 equal pieces. Shape each piece into a ball.

5 Roll out each ball into a 12 cm (5 inch) round. Drape one of the rounds over a baking dish and tuck the edge down around the mango slices. Repeat for the remaining tartlets. Chill until the dough is firm, 15 minutes. Heat the oven to 200°C (400°F, Gas 6). Bake the tartlets on the baking sheet, 20–25 minutes.

Dough is tucked down to seal in filling

Dough lid will become tartlet base

HOW TO MAKE PATE SUCREE DOUGH IN A FOOD PROCESSOR

Dough should form moist crumbs

1 Cut the butter into pieces. In a small bowl, mix the egg yolks with the vanilla essence. Put the flour in the food processor with the sugar and salt, and blend, about 5 seconds. Add the butter and work the mixture, using the pulse button, until the mixture resembles coarse crumbs, 10–15 seconds.

2 Add the egg yolk and vanilla essence mixture, and continue working the mixture until it resembles small peas, 25–30 seconds. If dough is dry, work in 15–30 ml (1–2 tbsp) water.

3 Transfer to a lightly floured work surface. Press into a ball and work with the heel of your hand until smooth. Chill until firm, about 30 minutes.

3 MAKE THE MANGO COULIS; UNMOULD THE TARTLETS

1 Make the mango coulis: put the reserved mango flesh into the food processor or a blender, and purée it.

2 Transfer the purée to a bowl; add the lime juice and stir it in. Taste the coulis and add icing sugar, if necessary. Chill.

3 Remove the tartlets from the oven when the crusts are golden brown. Let cool in the dishes, 2–3 minutes. To unmould, set a small plate on top of a baking dish; holding them firmly together, invert them. If any mango slices stick to the dish, remove with a palette knife and replace on the tartlet. Repeat for the remaining tartlets.

Use tea towel to handle hot baking dish

🍽 TO SERVE
Serve the tartlets at once. Accompany each tartlet with a lime twist, if you like. Pass the mango coulis separately.

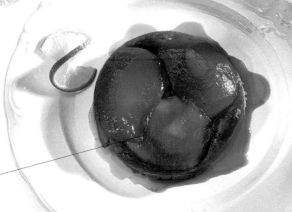

Caramel and mango are a perfect combination

V A R I A T I O N

CARAMELIZED UPSIDE-DOWN PEACH TART

Choose firm peaches so the fruit holds its shape during baking.

1 Omit the mangoes and coulis. Make and chill the dough as directed.
2 Make the caramel as directed, and pour it into the base of a 25 cm (10 inch) round baking dish. Let cool.
3 Immerse 1 kg (2 lb) peaches in boiling water, 10 seconds; transfer to a bowl of cold water. Cut 1 peach in half, using the indentation on one side as a guide. Twist with both hands to loosen the halves; then pull them apart. If the flesh clings, loosen it with a knife. Scoop out the stone and discard. Peel off the skin; cut peach halves lengthwise into two. Repeat for remaining peaches.
4 Tightly pack the peach wedges on top of the caramel, rounded-side down, in concentric circles.
5 On a lightly floured work surface, roll out the dough into a 28 cm (11 inch) round. Wrap it around the rolling pin and drape over the dish. Tuck the edge of the dough down around the peaches. Bake the tart as directed, allowing 30–35 minutes. Let the tart cool to tepid.
6 To unmould, set a platter on top of the baking dish. Hold dish and platter firmly together and invert them; remove the baking dish. Serve at once, cut into wedges.

TRIPLE-DECKER DRIED PEACH TART

Croustade Gasconne aux Pêches

 SERVES 6–8   WORK TIME 35–40 MINUTES*   BAKING TIME 55–60 MINUTES

EQUIPMENT

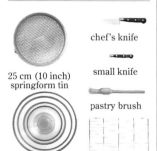

chef's knife

small knife

25 cm (10 inch) springform tin

pastry brush

bowls

wire rack

pastry scraper

saucepans

sieves

baking sheet

petal-shaped pastry cutter

rolling pin

metal skewer

aluminium foil

chopping board

In the Gascony region of southwestern France, dried fruit is popular eaten on its own. In this ideal winter dessert, dried peaches flavoured with peach liqueur are layered in a pastry case, which, in French, is called a croustade. *Lemon sorbet would be a delicious accompaniment.*

GETTING AHEAD

The dough can be prepared up to 2 days ahead and kept, tightly wrapped, in the refrigerator. The filling can be made up to 2 days ahead and kept in the refrigerator. Assemble and bake the tart not more than 8 hours before serving.

*plus 2–3 hours soaking and 30 minutes chilling

INGREDIENTS

dried peaches

sugar

plain flour

peach liqueur†

egg yolks

lemon juice

egg

unsalted butter

†Cognac can also be used

metric	SHOPPING LIST	imperial
250 g	dried peaches	8 oz
225 g	caster sugar	7 oz
	juice of 1/2 lemon	
30 ml	peach liqueur	2 tbsp
30 ml	unsalted butter	2 tbsp
	For the pâte brisée dough	
375 g	plain flour, more if needed	12 oz
175 g	unsalted butter, more for springform tin	6 oz
7.5 ml	salt	1 1/2 tsp
1	egg	1
2	egg yolks	2
15–30 ml	water, if needed	1–2 tbsp

ORDER OF WORK

1 SOAK THE PEACHES AND MAKE THE PATE BRISEE DOUGH

2 COOK PEACHES; LINE THE TIN; ASSEMBLE TART

1 SOAK THE PEACHES AND MAKE THE PATE BRISEE DOUGH

Dried peaches are quite leathery before soaking

1 Put the dried peaches on the chopping board. With the chef's knife, cut the dried peaches crosswise into pieces. Put the pieces into a medium bowl.

2 Pour enough boiling water over the peaches to cover them completely. Leave them to soak, 2–3 hours. While the peaches are soaking, make the pâte brisée dough.

Pinch butter with your fingertips to blend

4 Pound the butter with the rolling pin to soften it. Put the butter, salt, egg, and egg yolks into the well. With your fingertips, work the moist ingredients until thoroughly mixed.

3 Sift the flour onto the work surface. With your fingers, make a well in the centre of the flour.

7 Lightly flour the work surface. Blend the dough by pushing it away from you with the heel of your hand, then gathering it up, until it is very smooth and peels away from the work surface in one piece, 1–2 minutes. Shape into a ball, wrap, and chill, about 30 minutes.

5 Draw in the flour with the pastry scraper and work the flour into the other ingredients with your fingertips until coarse crumbs form.

6 If the dough crumbs are very dry, add 15–30 ml (1–2 tbsp) cold water. Press the dough into a ball. If it is sticky, work in a little more flour.

2 COOK PEACHES; LINE THE TIN; ASSEMBLE TART

1 Strain the peaches in a sieve, reserving the soaking liquid to help make up the cooking liquid for the peaches. Coarsely chop the peaches.

2 Put the 200 g (6 1/2 oz) sugar into a saucepan. Add the peach soaking liquid; heat until the sugar is dissolved. Add the peaches, and enough water to cover. Bring slowly to a boil and simmer, stirring occasionally, until tender, 20–25 minutes.

Drain, and discard any cooking liquid

3 Drain the peaches thoroughly. In a bowl, combine the peaches with the lemon juice and the peach liqueur. Brush the tin with melted butter.

4 Lightly flour the work surface and roll out one-third of the dough into a 37 cm (15 inch) round. Wrap the dough around the rolling pin and drape it over the tin. Lift the edge of the dough with one hand and let the dough fall into the bottom of the tin. Press it firmly against the bottom and side of the tin with the other hand. Spread one-third of the peaches over the bottom of the shell in an even layer.

Lift dough so it falls gently into tin

5 Divide the remaining dough into 3 portions. Roll out 1 portion and trim it to a 25 cm (10 inch) round, then set the round on top of the peaches.

6 Spread one-half of the remaining peaches over the dough round. Roll out a second portion of dough, trim it to a 25 cm (10 inch) round, and set the round on top of the peaches. Spread the remaining peaches over the dough round. Brush the dough on the side of the tin with cold water.

7 Roll out the third portion of dough and trim it to a 25 cm (10 inch) round. With the pastry cutter, cut out petal shapes close to the edge of the round. Brush the petals with a little cold water and press them gently onto the centre of the round, in a circle.

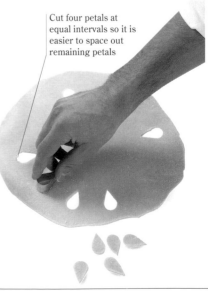

Cut four petals at equal intervals so it is easier to space out remaining petals

8 Carefully lift the dough round onto the final layer of peaches and press to seal it to the dough on the side of the tin. Trim the excess dough with the small knife and discard. Chill the tart, 30 minutes. Heat the oven to 190°C (375°F, Gas 5). Put the baking sheet in the oven to heat.

Remove trimmed dough to leave neat border

Petal cutouts are evenly spaced

9 Sprinkle the remaining sugar over the tart. Cut up the butter and dot over the top. Bake on the baking sheet until the metal skewer inserted in the centre for 30 seconds is hot to the touch when withdrawn, 55–60 minutes. If the tart browns too quickly, cover it loosely with foil and reduce the oven temperature to 180°C (350°F, Gas 4).

10 Transfer the peach tart to the wire rack and let cool slightly. Remove the side of the tin and let the tart cool completely.

¶○¶ TO SERVE
Slide the tart from the tin base onto a serving platter, cut it into wedges, and serve at room temperature.

Petal cutouts reveal tangy peach filling

Sugar bakes to a rustic finish

TRIPLE-DECKER PRUNE TART

Prunes take the place of dried peaches in this delicious tart. They are soaked in Armagnac – the mellow Gascon version of Cognac.

1 Omit the dried peaches, lemon juice, and peach liqueur.
2 Make and chill the pâte brisée dough as directed.
3 Cut 500 g (1 lb) moist pitted prunes in half and put them in a medium bowl. If the prunes are dry, first soak them in hot water, 15 minutes, then drain. Add 30 ml (2 tbsp) Armagnac and 15 ml (1 tbsp) sugar to the prunes, and mix.
4 Line the tin and layer the tart as directed, until you come to the third dough round. Stamp out 3 flower shapes from the round at equal intervals with a pastry cutter, and reserve. Set the dough round on top of the final layer of prunes. Trim as directed and reserve the trimmings.
5 Brush the tips of the flowers with a little cold water and lay them over the holes at different angles so that the prune filling is visible. Roll out the trimmings and stamp out 3 more flower shapes. Brush the bases of the flowers with cold water and press them onto the pastry round in between the flower cutouts. Bake the tart as directed.
6 Serve the tart cut into wedges, accompanied by custard sauce or vanilla ice cream, if you like.

FRESH MINCEMEAT TART

🍽 SERVES 8　🥄 WORK TIME 40–45 MINUTES*　🍲 BAKING TIME 40–45 MINUTES

EQUIPMENT

25 cm (10 inch) flan tin with removable base

grater

chef's knife

lemon squeezer

small knife

greaseproof paper

vegetable peeler

bowls

chopping board

melon baller

pastry brush

pastry blender †

pastry scraper

wire rack

metal skewer

rolling pin

baking sheet

† 2 round-bladed table knives can also be used

Mincemeat, originally a mixture of dried fruit, suet, spices, and a generous dash of alcohol, was developed to preserve meat. Here, fresh fruit is added to the traditional dried fruit and nut mixture to make a delicious filling for this tart.

*plus 1 hour chilling time

INGREDIENTS

plain flour

lemon

unsalted butter

Granny Smith apple

caster sugar

soft brown sugar

egg

whisky

chopped candied orange peel

vegetable shortening

slivered almonds

raisins

sultanas

seedless grapes

ground nutmeg

ground cinnamon

ground allspice

metric	SHOPPING LIST	imperial
1	Granny Smith apple	1
1	lemon	1
200 g	seedless grapes	6 1/2 oz
15 ml	chopped candied orange peel	1 tbsp
20 g	slivered almonds	3/4 oz
1.25 ml	each ground cinnamon, nutmeg, and allspice	1/4 tsp
90 g	each raisins and sultanas	3 oz
100 g	light soft brown sugar	3 1/4 oz
45 ml	whisky	3 tbsp
	whisky butter (see box, page 84) to serve (optional)	
	For the shortcrust pastry dough	
345 g	plain flour	11 oz
22.5 ml	caster sugar	1 1/2 tbsp
2.5 ml	salt	1/2 tsp
60 g	vegetable shortening	2 oz
90 g	unsalted butter, more for flan tin	3 oz
90–105 ml	cold water, more if needed	6–7 tbsp
1	egg, plus 2.5 ml (1/2 tsp) salt for glaze	1

ORDER OF WORK

1 MAKE THE SHORTCRUST PASTRY DOUGH; LINE THE TIN

2 MAKE THE FILLING AND LATTICE; BAKE THE TART

1 MAKE THE SHORTCRUST PASTRY DOUGH; LINE THE TIN

1 Make and chill the pastry dough (see box, page 12). Brush the tin with melted butter. Lightly flour the work surface and roll out two-thirds of the dough into a 30 cm (12 inch) round. Return the remaining dough to the refrigerator. Wrap the dough around the pin and drape it over the tin.

If draped gently, dough is not cut by sharp tin edge

2 Gently lift the edge of the dough with one hand, and press it well into the bottom of the tin with the other hand, pressing to seal any cracks. Overlap the dough slightly inside the rim of the tin.

3 Roll the rolling pin over the top of the tin, pressing down to cut off the excess dough. Press the dough trimmings into the remaining dough.

4 With your thumbs, press the dough evenly up the tin side to increase the height of the shell. Chill the shell until firm, about 15 minutes. Meanwhile, make the filling.

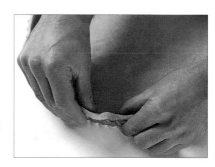

2 MAKE THE FILLING AND LATTICE; BAKE THE TART

Lemon juice adds piquancy to filling

2 Grate the zest from the lemon onto a sheet of greaseproof paper. Halve the lemon and squeeze the juice. With the small knife, cut the grapes lengthwise in half.

1 Peel the apple and cut out the flower and stalk ends. Halve the apple, then scoop out the core. Set each apple half cut-side down and cut horizontally into 1 cm ($^3/_8$ inch) slices. Cut the slices lengthwise into 1 cm ($^3/_8$ inch) strips. Gather the strips together and cut crosswise into cubes.

3 Put the apple, grapes, lemon zest and juice, candied orange peel, almonds, ground cinnamon, nutmeg, and allspice, raisins, sultanas, sugar, and whisky into a bowl. Stir to combine.

4 Spoon the fresh mincemeat over the bottom of the pastry shell and gently press it down with the back of a spoon.

Whisky accents flavour of dried and fresh fruit

5 Make the egg glaze: lightly beat the egg with the salt. Roll out the remaining dough and trim it to a 26.25 cm (10 ½ inch) square. Using the small knife, cut into 2 cm (¾ inch) strips. There should be 14 strips.

6 Lay 7 strips crosswise over the filling, about 2 cm (¾ inch) apart, letting the ends hang over the edge of the tin. Fold back alternate strips halfway. Set an eighth strip across the centre of the unfolded strips. Unfold the folded strips to cover the crosswise strip, again leaving ends to hang over the edge of the tin. Fold back alternate strips.

Avoid stretching strips of dough

WHISKY BUTTER

Whisky butter is a simple variation of brandy butter, the traditional accompaniment to Christmas pudding.

🍽 SERVES 8

🍲 WORK TIME 15 MINUTES

❄ CHILLING TIME 1–2 HOURS

metric	SHOPPING LIST	imperial
125 g	unsalted butter	4 oz
100 g	caster sugar	3¼ oz
60 ml	whisky	2 fl oz

1 Using an electric mixer, beat the butter until creamy. Add the sugar and continue beating until light and fluffy, 2–3 minutes. Beat in the whisky, 1 spoonful at a time. Chill the sauce until set, 1–2 hours.

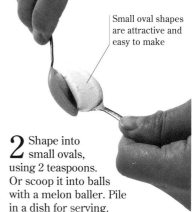

Small oval shapes are attractive and easy to make

2 Shape into small ovals, using 2 teaspoons. Or scoop it into balls with a melon baller. Pile in a dish for serving.

FESTIVE MINCEMEAT TART

The mincemeat in this festive tart is made with dried fruit.

7 Place the ninth strip about 2 cm (³/₄ inch) from the eighth. Continue until half of the surface is latticed. Turn the tin and repeat the process on the other half of the tart.

8 Brush the ends of the strips with cold water. With your fingertips, seal the strips to the pastry shell, pinching off the overhanging ends. Brush the lattice with the egg glaze.

9 Chill until firm, about 15 minutes. Heat the oven to 180°C (350°F, Gas 4). Put the baking sheet in the oven to heat. Bake on the baking sheet until lightly browned, and the metal skewer inserted in the centre of the mincemeat for 30 seconds is hot to the touch when withdrawn, 40–45 minutes. Let cool slightly on wire rack; set on a bowl to loosen and remove side.

Side of flan tin falls easily from tart when base is set on bowl

Lattice decoration displays filling of mincemeat

🍽 TO SERVE
Slide the tart from the tin base onto a serving platter. Cut the tart into wedges and serve with whisky butter, if you like.

1 Omit the apple and grapes. Make and chill the shortcrust pastry dough, and line the flan tin as directed. Grate the lemon zest and squeeze the juice.
2 Chop 100 g (3¼ oz) each dried figs, dried dates, and dried apricots. Combine the chopped fruit, raisins, sultanas, lemon zest and juice, chopped candied orange peel, almonds, spices, sugar, and whisky. Spoon the filling over the bottom of the pastry shell and brush the edge of the shell with cold water. Roll out the remaining dough into a 28 cm (11 inch) round. Fold the dough into quarters.
3 Cut 2.5 cm (1 inch) diagonal incisions across folds of dough. This will make "V" shapes when the dough is unfolded.
4 Unfold the dough, wrap it around the rolling pin, and drape it over the filling. Roll the rolling pin over the tin edge to trim the top crust even with the bottom crust. Press the crusts together to seal, then brush the top with egg glaze. Chill, bake, unmould, and serve as directed.

GETTING AHEAD
The mincemeat can be made up to 2 weeks ahead and kept, covered, in the refrigerator. The dough can be made up to 2 days ahead and kept, tightly wrapped, in the refrigerator. Assemble and bake the tart not more than 8 hours ahead.

FLAKY PEAR TARTLETS

 SERVES 8   WORK TIME 1¼–1½ HOURS*   BAKING TIME 30–40 MINUTES

EQUIPMENT

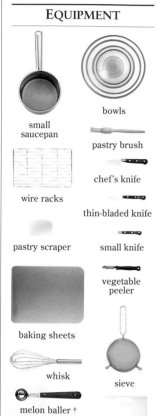

small saucepan

bowls

pastry brush

chef's knife

wire racks

thin-bladed knife

pastry scraper

small knife

vegetable peeler

baking sheets

whisk

sieve

melon baller †

wooden spoon

palette knife

chopping board

rolling pin

† teaspoon or small knife can also be used

These tartlets are a party favourite of mine – a spectacular contrast of hot and cold, they need little last-minute preparation. If you wish, you can save 40–50 minutes work time by substituting 500 g (1 lb) ready-prepared puff pastry dough for the homemade dough used in the recipe.
*plus 1¼ hours chilling time

INGREDIENTS

pears

double cream

plain flour

vanilla essence

unsalted butter

egg

caster sugar

lemon juice

icing sugar

metric	SHOPPING LIST	imperial
4	pears, total weight about 1½ lb	4
	juice of 1 lemon	
50 g	sugar	1¾ oz
	For the caramel sauce	
125 ml	water	4 fl oz
150 g	caster sugar	5 oz
125 ml	double cream	4 fl oz
	For the puff pastry dough	
250 g	plain flour	8 oz
250 g	unsalted butter, more for baking sheet	8 oz
5 ml	salt	1 tsp
5 ml	lemon juice	1 tsp
150 ml	water, more if needed	¼ pint
1	egg, plus 2.5 ml (½ tsp) salt for glaze	1
	For the Chantilly cream	
125 ml	double cream	4 fl oz
5–10 ml	icing sugar	1–2 tsp
2.5 ml	vanilla essence	½ tsp

ORDER OF WORK

1 MAKE AND BAKE THE PUFF PASTRY CASES

2 MAKE THE SAUCE AND THE CHANTILLY CREAM

3 PREPARE THE PEAR FANS

4 GRILL THE PEAR FANS AND ASSEMBLE THE TARTLETS

1 MAKE AND BAKE THE PUFF PASTRY CASES

Cut cleanly through dough from tip to heel of knife blade

1 Make and chill the puff pastry dough (see pages 104–105). Sprinkle 2 baking sheets with cold water. Lightly flour the work surface, then roll out the puff pastry dough, and trim it to a 20 x 50 cm (8 x 20 inch) rectangle.

2 Cut the dough in half lengthwise. Cut diagonally at 10 cm (4 inch) intervals along the length of each piece of dough to make 8 diamond shapes.

3 Transfer the pastry dough shapes to the baking sheets and press them down lightly. Beat the egg with the salt just until mixed, then brush the dough with the glaze.

4 With the tip of the small knife, mark lines parallel to the edges of each one, cutting halfway through the dough to form a lid. Chill until firm, about 15 minutes. Heat the oven to 220°C (425°F, Gas 7).

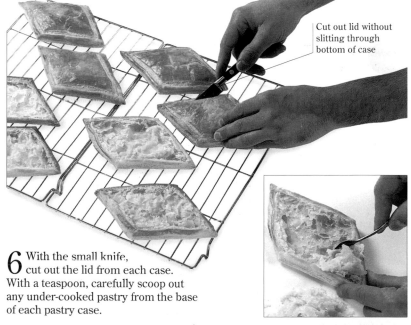

Cut out lid without slitting through bottom of case

5 Bake the cases in the heated oven until they have started to brown, about 15 minutes. Reduce the oven temperature to 190°C (375°F, Gas 5), and continue baking until golden and crisp, 20–25 minutes longer, reversing level of baking sheets halfway through cooking. Transfer to wire racks to cool.

6 With the small knife, cut out the lid from each case. With a teaspoon, carefully scoop out any under-cooked pastry from the base of each pastry case.

2 MAKE THE SAUCE AND THE CHANTILLY CREAM

1 Put the water in the saucepan, add the sugar, and cook over low heat, stirring occasionally, until the sugar has dissolved. Boil, without stirring, until the syrup starts to turn golden. Lower the heat and swirl the saucepan once or twice so that the syrup colours evenly.

Do not stir during boiling or sugar may crystallize

2 Remove the saucepan from the heat and let the bubbles subside. Immediately pour in the cream, stirring to mix. Heat gently until the caramel has dissolved. Leave the sauce to cool.

! TAKE CARE !
The caramel will splutter, so stand at arm's length when pouring.

3 Make the Chantilly cream: pour the double cream into a chilled bowl and whip until soft peaks form. Add the icing sugar and vanilla essence, and continue whipping until stiff peaks form. Chill.

3 PREPARE THE PEAR FANS

1 Butter a baking sheet. Peel the pears. Cut out the flower ends with the small knife. Halve the pears, cut out the stalk ends, then scoop out the cores with the melon baller or with a teaspoon or small knife.

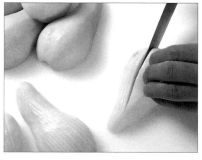

2 Set 1 pear half, cut-side down, on the chopping board. Using the thin-bladed knife, cut it lengthwise into thin slices, keeping the slices attached at the stalk end. Repeat with the remaining pear halves.

3 With your fingers, flatten the slices of 1 pear half to form a fan. Transfer the pear fan to the prepared baking sheet, using the palette knife and your fingertips. Repeat with the remaining pear halves.

Buttered baking sheet keeps pears from sticking during cooking

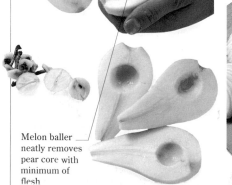

Melon baller neatly removes pear core with minimum of flesh

4 Brush each pear fan with the lemon juice. If preparing ahead, cover the pear fans tightly and chill.

! TAKE CARE !
Be sure that the pear slices are well coated with lemon juice so they do not discolour on standing.

4 GRILL THE PEAR FANS AND ASSEMBLE THE TARTLETS

1 Heat the grill. Sprinkle the pear fans with the sugar. Grill about 7.5–10 cm (3–4 inches) from the heat until caramelized, 3–5 minutes.

2 Transfer the pastry cases to individual plates; spoon a little Chantilly cream into each. Transfer the pear fans to the pastry cases. Drizzle a little cool caramel sauce over each serving and partially cover each pear fan with a pastry lid.

Spoon Chantilly cream evenly into case

Caramel sauce drizzles easily off spoon

🍴 TO SERVE
Serve at once while the pear fans are hot and the Chantilly cream is cold. Serve the remaining caramel sauce separately.

Caramel sauce adds sweetness

Crisp puff pastry is a classic container for Chantilly cream topped with grilled pear fan

FLAKY APPLE TARTLETS
Caramelized apple fans replace pear fans in this version of Flaky Pear Tartlets, and sit on Chantilly cream in golden puff pastry rounds.

1 Omit the pears. Make and chill the dough as directed. Roll out the dough; trim it to a 20 x 50 cm (8 x 20 inch) rectangle as directed. Cut rounds with a 10 cm (4 inch) fluted pastry cutter and brush with egg glaze. With a 7.5 cm (3 inch) fluted cutter or the tip of a small knife, mark a circle on each round, cutting halfway through the dough. Bake, and cut out the lids as directed.
2 Make sauce and Chantilly cream as directed.
3 Peel 4 Granny Smith apples and prepare and grill in the same way as the pear fans. Put the chilled Chantilly cream and grilled apple fans in the cases as directed. Cover with the lids and serve at once. Serve the sauce separately.

GETTING AHEAD
The pastry cases can be baked up to 2 days ahead and stored in an airtight container. Make the caramel sauce and Chantilly cream, and prepare the pears not more than 2 hours ahead. Grill the pears and assemble the tartlets just before serving.

FIG AND MULLED WINE TART

 SERVES 6–8   WORK TIME 25–30 MINUTES*   BAKING TIME 15–20 MINUTES

EQUIPMENT

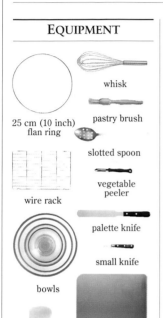

whisk

25 cm (10 inch) flan ring

pastry brush

slotted spoon

vegetable peeler

wire rack

palette knife

small knife

bowls

pastry scraper

baking sheet

saucepans, 1 with lid, 1 heavy-based with lid

rolling pin

sieve

plastic bag

rubber spatula

Fresh figs, with their deep red flesh and delicate flavour, call for the simplest treatment. Here, they are poached briefly in mulled wine syrup.

*plus 1¼ hours chilling time

INGREDIENTS

figs

black peppercorns

dry red wine

milk

orange

whole nutmeg

egg yolks

lemon

unsalted butter

vanilla pod†

plain flour

caster sugar

cinnamon stick

whole cloves

double cream

egg

fine yellow cornmeal

†2.5 ml (½ tsp) vanilla essence can also be used

metric	SHOPPING LIST	imperial
500 g	purple figs	1 lb
1	orange	1
1	lemon	1
1	piece of whole nutmeg	1
100 g	caster sugar	3¼ oz
1	5 cm (2 inch) piece of cinnamon stick	1
2	whole cloves	2
5 ml	black peppercorns	1 tsp
500 ml	dry red wine	16 fl oz
For the cornmeal pastry dough		
125 g	plain flour, more if needed	4 oz
45 g	fine yellow cornmeal	1½ oz
75 g	unsalted butter, more for baking sheet and flan ring	2½ oz
1	egg	1
50 g	caster sugar	1¾ oz
1.25 ml	salt	¼ tsp
For the lightened pastry cream		
½	vanilla pod	½
250 ml	milk	8 fl oz
3	egg yolks	3
45 ml	caster sugar	3 tbsp
30 ml	flour	2 tbsp
10 ml	unsalted butter	2 tsp
90 ml	double cream	3 fl oz

ORDER OF WORK

1. **MAKE THE DOUGH, LINE THE FLAN RING, AND BAKE THE ROUND**

2. **MAKE THE LIGHTENED PASTRY CREAM**

3. **MAKE THE SYRUP; POACH THE FIGS; ASSEMBLE TART**

1 MAKE THE DOUGH, LINE THE FLAN RING, AND BAKE THE ROUND

Use pastry scraper to pull ingredients together

1 Sift the flour onto the work surface. Add the cornmeal and make a well in the centre. Pound the butter with the rolling pin to soften it.

2 Beat the egg to mix. Put the butter, egg, sugar, and salt into the well. With your fingertips, work these ingredients until thoroughly mixed.

3 Draw in the flour and cornmeal with the pastry scraper, and work them into the other ingredients with your fingers until coarse crumbs form. Press the dough into a ball. If it is sticky, work in a little more flour.

Blend dough with heel of hand

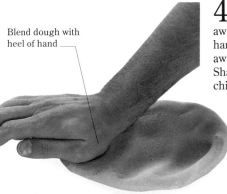

4 Lightly flour the work surface. Blend the dough by pushing it away from you with the heel of your hand, then gathering it up, until it peels away from the surface, 1–2 minutes. Shape into a ball, wrap it tightly, and chill until firm, about 30 minutes.

5 Set the flan ring on baking sheet. Brush both with melted butter. Roll out dough on a floured surface into a 28 cm (11 inch) round. Wrap around rolling pin, and drape over ring.

Flan ring keeps dough in neat round

6 Gently lift the edge of the dough with one hand, and press it well into the bottom edge of the flan ring with the other hand. Fold over the excess dough inside the flan ring to form a border to the pastry round. Chill until firm, about 15 minutes. Heat the oven to 190°C (375°F, Gas 5).

7 Bake the pastry round in the heated oven until set and golden brown, 15–20 minutes. Carefully slide the pastry round onto the wire rack, lift off the flan ring, and let cool.

2 MAKE THE LIGHTENED PASTRY CREAM

While folding, bowl is turned anticlockwise

1 Split the vanilla pod, if using. In the heavy-based pan, bring the milk to a boil with the pod. Remove from the heat, cover, and let stand, 10–15 minutes. Whisk the egg yolks and sugar until thick, 2–3 minutes. Stir in flour. Gradually stir in the hot milk until smooth. Pour back into the pan. Bring to a boil over medium heat, whisking constantly until thickened.

! TAKE CARE !
If lumps form, remove from the heat at once and whisk until smooth again.

2 Lower the heat, and cook, still whisking, until the pastry cream softens slightly, about 2 minutes. Remove from heat, take out vanilla pod, if using, or stir in vanilla essence. Transfer to a bowl, rub the butter over surface of the cream to keep it from forming a skin, and chill, 30 minutes.

ANNE SAYS
"Simmering the pastry cream cooks the flour so it leaves no aftertaste."

3 Pour the double cream into a chilled bowl and whip until soft peaks form; cover and chill. Add the cream to the chilled pastry cream and fold together gently but thoroughly, scooping under the pastry cream and turning the mixture over in a rolling motion. Cover and chill. Meanwhile, make the syrup and poach the figs.

3 MAKE THE SYRUP; POACH THE FIGS; ASSEMBLE TART

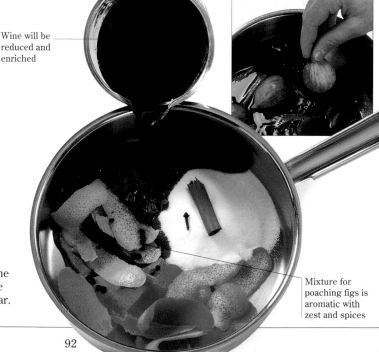

Wine will be reduced and enriched

1 Prick each fig 2 or 3 times with the tines of a fork so that the syrup will penetrate the fruit.

2 Pare the zest from the orange and lemon. Crush the nutmeg in the plastic bag with the rolling pin. Put the zest and nutmeg into a saucepan with the sugar, spices, and peppercorns. Add the wine. Heat, stirring, to dissolve the sugar. Bring just to a boil, then add the figs.

Mixture for poaching figs is aromatic with zest and spices

3 Cover, and poach just until the figs are tender, 3–5 minutes. Remove the figs with the slotted spoon, allowing them to drain well, and let cool. Continue simmering the syrup until reduced to about 125 ml (4 fl oz), 25–30 minutes. Strain, and let cool.

Mulled wine syrup adds rich colour

Leave figs attached at flower end

4 Cut off the stalks from the figs; cut the figs into quarters, leaving them attached at the flower ends. Slide the pastry round onto a serving plate.

5 Spread the pastry cream over the pastry round. Arrange the figs in concentric circles on top, and pull each one open slightly. Spoon 15–30 ml (1–2 tbsp) of the syrup over the figs.

🍽 **TO SERVE**
Just before serving, spoon the remaining syrup over the tart. Serve at room temperature, cut into wedges.

Poached figs are tender and full of flavour

VARIATION

FIG AND MULLED WINE TARTLETS

Sliced figs top individual tartlets in this version of Fig and Mulled Wine Tart.

1 Make and chill the cornmeal pastry dough as directed. Brush a baking sheet with melted butter. Lightly flour the work surface. With your hands, shape the dough into a cylinder about 30 cm (12 inches) long. Cut the cylinder into 6 equal pieces. Shape each piece into a ball, then roll out each ball into a 12 cm (5 inch) round.
2 Set the rounds on the baking sheet and fold over the edge of each round to form a border. Chill until firm, about 15 minutes. Bake the rounds in the oven until golden brown, 12–15 minutes; cool on a wire rack.
3 Make the pastry cream and lighten it as directed. Make the mulled wine syrup and reduce as directed.
4 Transfer the pastry rounds to individual plates and spread the lightened pastry cream on each one.
5 Do not poach the figs. Cut them lengthwise into thin slices. Overlap in a petal pattern on each tartlet.
6 Brush the fig slices with the syrup; serve any remaining syrup separately.

GETTING AHEAD
The dough can be made up to 2 days ahead and kept, tightly wrapped, in the refrigerator. You can bake the pastry round up to 8 hours ahead; poach the figs and make the lightened pastry cream up to 2 hours ahead. The tart should not be assembled until just before serving.

MISSISSIPPI MUD PIE

EQUIPMENT

- ice cream maker
- piping bag and medium star nozzle
- wooden spoon
- whisk
- sieves
- bowls
- food processor†
- pastry brush
- chef's knife
- 23 cm (9 inch) pie dish
- chopping board
- rubber spatula
- wire rack
- saucepans, 1 heavy-based

- baking sheet

†rolling pin and plastic bag can also be used

In this popular American dessert, a chocolate crumb crust is filled with homemade coffee ice cream swirled with chocolate, then piped with cream, and served with hot fudge sauce.

GETTING AHEAD

The pie and fudge sauce can be made up to 3 days ahead. The pie should be kept, tightly wrapped, in the freezer and the fudge sauce kept, covered, in the refrigerator.

plus 15 minutes chilling and 25–30 minutes baking

INGREDIENTS

- caster sugar
- chocolate biscuits
- egg yolks
- unsalted butter
- milk
- dark rum
- cocoa powder
- soft brown sugar
- whole blanched almonds
- double cream
- instant coffee granules
- cornflour

ANNE SAYS
"Choose plain chocolate-flavoured, not chocolate-coated, biscuits."

ORDER OF WORK

1. **PREPARE THE COFFEE CUSTARD; MAKE AND BAKE THE CRUMB CRUST**

2. **TOAST THE ALMONDS; MAKE THE FUDGE SAUCE**

3. **FREEZE THE ICE CREAM AND PIE**

4. **FINISH THE PIE**

metric	SHOPPING LIST	imperial
	For the coffee ice cream	
600 ml	milk	1 pint
45 ml	instant coffee granules	3 tbsp
135 g	caster sugar	4½ oz
8	egg yolks	8
30 ml	cornflour	2 tbsp
250 ml	double cream	8 fl oz
	For the chocolate crumb crust	
125 g	unsalted butter, more for pie dish	4 oz
250 g	plain dark crisp chocolate biscuits	8 oz
45 ml	caster sugar	3 tbsp
	For the fudge sauce	
60 g	whole blanched almonds	2 oz
150 ml	double cream	¼ pint
60 g	unsalted butter	2 oz
100 g	caster sugar	3¼ oz
135 g	light soft brown sugar	4½ oz
90 g	cocoa powder	3 oz
	salt	
15 ml	dark rum, more to taste	1 tbsp
175 ml	double cream for decoration	6 fl oz

1 PREPARE THE COFFEE CUSTARD; MAKE AND BAKE THE CRUMB CRUST

Whisk while pouring

1 Put the milk in a medium heavy-based saucepan with the instant coffee granules and bring just to a boil, stirring until the coffee granules have dissolved. Set aside one-quarter of the milk mixture. Stir the sugar into the remaining mixture until dissolved.

2 In a medium bowl, whisk the egg yolks with the cornflour. Add the sweetened hot milk mixture and whisk just until smooth.

3 Pour the custard back into the saucepan and cook over medium heat, stirring constantly, just until it comes to a boil and thickens enough to coat the back of a spoon. Your finger will leave a clear trail across the spoon. Custard may curdle if cooked longer.

4 Off the heat, stir in the reserved milk until thoroughly combined. Strain the custard into a cold bowl and cover tightly to prevent a skin forming on the surface. Let cool.

Coarse chocolate biscuit crumbs will make crisp pie crust

6 Press the crumbs evenly over the bottom and up the side of the pie dish. Chill until firm, 15 minutes. Heat the oven to 180°C (350°F, Gas 4). Put the baking sheet in the oven to heat.

5 Melt the butter. Brush the pie dish with melted butter. Grind the biscuits to coarse crumbs in the food processor, using the pulse button. Transfer to a bowl and add the melted butter and sugar. Stir until all the crumbs are moistened.

Melted butter will bind crumbs and sugar

7 Bake the crumb crust on the baking sheet in the heated oven, 15 minutes. Let cool on the wire rack. The crust will harden as it cools.

2 TOAST THE ALMONDS; MAKE THE FUDGE SAUCE

1 Coarsely chop the almonds. Spread them on the baking sheet; toast in the heated oven, stirring occasionally, until lightly browned, 10–12 minutes.

2 In a medium saucepan, heat the double cream and butter, stirring occasionally, until the butter melts and the mixture comes just to a boil. Add the sugars and stir them in until dissolved.

Whisk constantly so sauce does not scorch

Cocoa powder gives fudge sauce rich chocolate flavour

3 Sift the cocoa. Whisk it, with a pinch of salt, into the cream and sugar mixture, and bring back to a boil. Gently simmer the fudge sauce, whisking constantly, until the cocoa powder has dissolved, 1–2 minutes longer. Stir in rum.

4 Transfer 125 ml (4 fl oz) of the fudge sauce to a bowl and combine with half the almonds. Let cool. Set the remaining sauce and almonds aside.

3 FREEZE THE ICE CREAM AND PIE

1 If the custard has formed a skin, whisk to dissolve it. Pour the coffee custard into the ice cream maker and freeze until slushy, following the manufacturer's directions. Meanwhile, chill 2 large bowls in the freezer.

2 Pour the cream into one of the chilled bowls, and whisk until soft peaks form. Add the cream to the half-set custard and continue freezing in the ice cream maker until firm. Freezing time varies with the machine used.

Add whipped cream when ice cream is half set

3 Transfer the coffee ice cream to the second chilled bowl. Add the cooled almond fudge mixture. With 2 round-bladed table knives, cut in the mixture until partly mixed.

ANNE SAYS
"Return the ice cream to the freezer if it starts to melt, otherwise it will seep into the crumb crust."

4 Spread the coffee ice cream and almond fudge mixture over the bottom of the crumb crust. Swirl the top with the back of a metal spoon and freeze, at least 1–2 hours, or up to 3 days.

Use back of spoon to make swirls in ice cream

4 FINISH THE PIE

1 If the pie has been frozen for more than 12 hours, let it soften in the refrigerator, 1 hour. Pour the double cream into a chilled bowl and whip until it forms stiff peaks.

2 Put the cream into the piping bag fitted with a medium star nozzle, and pipe rosettes around the edge of the pie. Sprinkle over the reserved almonds. Reheat the fudge sauce.

🍽️ TO SERVE
Transfer the pie dish to a serving platter. Serve the pie directly from the dish, cut into wedges. Drizzle hot fudge sauce over the top of each serving, and serve at once.

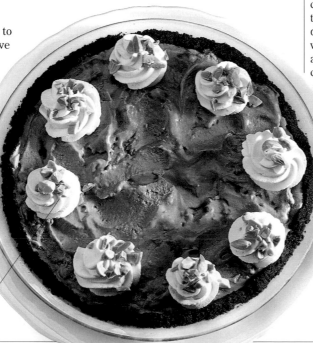

Almond-studded cream rosettes crown ice cream pie

V A R I A T I O N
GINGERNUT ICE CREAM PIE

Gingernut biscuits replace the chocolate biscuits, and ginger ice cream fills the pie.

1 Omit the instant coffee granules, chocolate biscuits, blanched almonds, and rum. Grind or crush 250 g (8 oz) gingernut biscuits, then make the crumb crust, line the pie dish, and bake the crumb crust as directed.
2 Finely chop 30 ml (2 tbsp) crystallized ginger. Make the custard as directed, transfer to a bowl, then stir in 5 ml (1 tsp) ground ginger with the chopped ginger. Set the custard aside to cool. Make the fudge sauce as directed, stirring in 2.5 ml (1/2 tsp) vanilla essence in place of the rum. Set aside 125 ml (4 fl oz) of the sauce to cool. Set the remaining sauce aside.
3 Freeze the ice cream as directed; swirl in the cooled fudge sauce. Spread the ice cream mixture in the shell; freeze as directed.
4 Whip the cream. Pipe swirls and stars of cream around the pie. Reheat the fudge sauce.
5 Serve the pie and fudge sauce as directed.

BAVARIAN PLUM TART

 SERVES 8–10 WORK TIME 35–40 MINUTES* BAKING TIME 50–55 MINUTES

EQUIPMENT

28 cm (11 inch) fluted quiche dish

 sieve

 pastry brush

small knife

 baking sheet

ladle

 wire rack

bowls

 pastry scraper

 whisk

rolling pin

Bavaria is famous for its cakes and tarts. In this recipe, a quick version of brioche forms the base for a plum tart. Juice from the fruit mingles with the custard filling to bring about a deliciously moist result. The amount of sugar you need depends on the sweetness of the plums. Apricots, or greengages, are also delicious in this tart.

*plus 2¼–3 hours total rising time

INGREDIENTS

purple plums

unsalted butter

yeast

dried breadcrumbs

plain flour

eggs

egg yolks

double cream

caster sugar

vegetable oil

metric	SHOPPING LIST	imperial
875 g	purple plums	1¾ lb
30 ml	dried breadcrumbs	2 tbsp
2	egg yolks	2
100 g	caster sugar, more if needed	3¼ oz
60 ml	double cream	2 fl oz
	For the brioche dough	
7.5 ml	dried yeast, or 9 g (⅓ oz) fresh yeast	1½ tsp
60 ml	lukewarm water	2 fl oz
	vegetable oil for bowl	
375 g	plain flour, more if needed	12 oz
30 ml	caster sugar	2 tbsp
5 ml	salt	1 tsp
3	eggs	3
125 g	unsalted butter, more for quiche dish	4 oz

ORDER OF WORK

1 MAKE THE BRIOCHE DOUGH; STONE THE PLUMS

2 LINE THE DISH AND FILL THE DOUGH SHELL

3 MAKE THE CUSTARD AND FINISH THE TART

1 MAKE THE BRIOCHE DOUGH; STONE THE PLUMS

1 Sprinkle or crumble the yeast over the water in a small bowl. Let stand until dissolved, 5 minutes. Lightly oil a medium bowl. Sift the flour onto the work surface. Make a well in the centre and add the sugar, salt, yeast mixture, and eggs.

Circle of flour holds in wet ingredients

2 With your fingertips, work the ingredients in the well until they are thoroughly mixed. Draw in the flour with the pastry scraper.

3 Work the flour into the other ingredients with your fingertips to form a soft dough; work in more flour if it is very sticky.

Lifting dough is integral part of kneading process

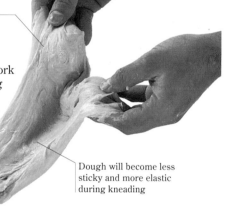

4 Knead the dough on a floured work surface, lifting it up and throwing it down until it is very elastic and resembles chamois leather, about 10 minutes. Work in more flour as necessary, so that, at the end of kneading, the dough is slightly sticky but peels easily from the work surface.

Dough will become less sticky and more elastic during kneading

5 Pound the butter with the rolling pin to soften it. Add the butter to the dough; pinch and squeeze to mix it in, then knead the dough on the work surface until it is smooth, 3–5 minutes. Alternatively, the dough can be kneaded and the butter added using an electric mixer with a dough hook.

Brioche dough should be satiny smooth

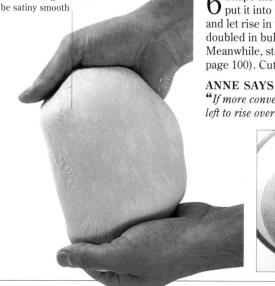

6 Shape the dough into a ball and put it into the oiled bowl. Cover, and let rise in the refrigerator until doubled in bulk, 1½–2 hours. Meanwhile, stone the plums (see box, page 100). Cut each plum half into two.

ANNE SAYS
"If more convenient, the dough can be left to rise overnight in the refrigerator."

HOW TO HALVE AND STONE PLUMS

The riper the fruit, the more easily it separates from the stone.

1 With a small sharp knife, cut plum in half, following the indentation on one side as a guide.

2 Twist with both hands to loosen the plum halves; then pull them apart.

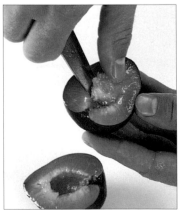

3 If the flesh clings, loosen it with the knife. Scoop out the stone with the point of the knife; discard.

2 LINE THE DISH AND FILL THE DOUGH SHELL

1 Brush the quiche dish with melted butter. Knead the chilled brioche dough lightly to knock out the air. Flour the work surface; roll out the dough into a 32 cm (13 inch) round.

Dough is easy to drape with help of rolling pin

2 Wrap the dough around the rolling pin and loosely drape it over the quiche dish.

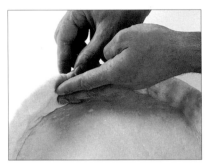

3 Lift the edge of the dough with one hand and press it well into bottom and up side of dish with other hand.

4 With the small knife, trim off the excess dough, using the rim of the dish as a guide.

Plum wedges will be arranged cut-side up to help excess juice evaporate

5 Sprinkle the breadcrumbs over the bottom of the dough shell. Arrange the plum wedges, cut-side up, in concentric circles on top. Let stand at room temperature until the edge of the dough is puffed, 30–45 minutes. Meanwhile, heat the oven to 220°C (425°F, Gas 7). Put the baking sheet in the oven to heat.

ANNE SAYS
"Breadcrumbs absorb juice from the fruit so the brioche does not become soggy."

3 MAKE THE CUSTARD AND FINISH THE TART

1 Put the egg yolks and two-thirds of the sugar into a bowl. Pour in the double cream. Whisk the mixture together to combine.

2 Sprinkle the plum wedges with the remaining sugar and bake the tart on the baking sheet, 5 minutes. Reduce the heat to 180°C (350°F, Gas 4).

3 Ladle the custard mixture over the fruit, return the tart to the oven, and continue baking until the dough is browned, the fruit is tender, and the custard is set, 45–50 minutes longer.

! TAKE CARE !
Do not overbake the tart or the custard may curdle.

Sugared plums cook to a shiny glaze

🍴 TO SERVE
Let the tart cool on the wire rack. Serve the tart warm or at room temperature, cut into wedges.

BAVARIAN BLUEBERRY TART

Traditionally, bilberries would be used for this tart in Bavaria. Here, blueberries are used because they are more readily available.

1 Omit the plums. Prepare the brioche dough as directed. Pick over 500 g (1 lb) blueberries; wash only if dirty. Leave the fruit whole.
2 Assemble the tart as directed. Make custard as directed, using 60 g (2 oz) sugar, 4 egg yolks, and 125 ml (4 fl oz) double cream.
3 Sprinkle the blueberries with 30 ml (2 tbsp) sugar. Bake the tart, 5 minutes, as directed. Ladle the custard over the blueberries and bake, 45–50 minutes longer.
4 Just before serving, use a sieve to sprinkle the tart with 15–30 ml (1–2 tbsp) icing sugar. Serve the blueberry tart warm or at room temperature, cut into neat wedges.

—— GETTING AHEAD ——
The brioche dough can be prepared up to 1 day ahead and kept, covered, in the refrigerator. The tart is best eaten on the day of baking.

APPLE JALOUSIE

EQUIPMENT

rolling pin

chef's knife

pastry brush

large frying pan †

melon baller

vegetable peeler

small knife

wire rack

pastry scraper

baking sheet

medium sieve

chopping board

small sieve

whisk

wooden spoon

† large sauté pan can also be used

ANNE SAYS
"*Puff pastry dough must be kept cold, so a marble slab is the ideal surface for rolling out. Alternatively, place a tray of ice cubes on your work surface for 15 minutes, and dry before rolling out dough.*"

In France, a jalousie *is a louvred shutter – perfect for the observance of wives by jealous husbands. In this golden pastry, the top layer of dough is slashed crosswise to look like a shutter, revealing glimpses of the apple compote inside. The filling is spiced with fresh root ginger and the flavour is best when tart dessert apples, such as Granny Smith, are used.*

GETTING AHEAD
The puff pastry dough can be given 4 turns, tightly wrapped, and refrigerated up to 2 days, or frozen up to 3 months. Complete the final 2 turns and bake the day of serving.

*plus 1¼ hours chilling time

metric	SHOPPING LIST	imperial
1 kg	Granny Smith apples	2 lb
2.5 cm	piece of fresh root ginger	1 inch
15 ml	unsalted butter	1 tbsp
100 g	caster sugar	3¼ oz
1	egg white	1
For the puff pastry dough		
250 g	plain flour	8 oz
250 g	unsalted butter	8 oz
5 ml	salt	1 tsp
5 ml	lemon juice	1 tsp
125 ml	water, more if needed	4 fl oz

INGREDIENTS

Granny Smith apples

fresh root ginger

unsalted butter

plain flour

caster sugar

egg white

lemon juice

ANNE SAYS
"*If you are short of time, you can save 40–50 minutes work time by substituting 500 g (1 lb) ready-prepared puff pastry dough for the homemade puff pastry dough used in the recipe.*"

ORDER OF WORK

1 MAKE THE PUFF PASTRY DOUGH; PREPARE THE FILLING

2 ASSEMBLE AND BAKE THE JALOUSIE

1 MAKE THE PUFF PASTRY DOUGH; PREPARE THE FILLING

1 Make and chill the puff pastry dough (see pages 104–105). Peel the apples with the vegetable peeler. Cut out the flower and stalk ends from each apple.

Minimum of apple flesh is removed with vegetable peeler

2 Halve the apples with the chef's knife, then scoop out the core from each half with the melon baller.

3 Set 1 apple half, cut-side down, on the chopping board. Cut it horizontally into 5 mm (1/4 inch) slices.

4 Cut the slices lengthwise into 5 mm (1/4 inch) strips. Gather the strips in a pile and cut across into dice. Repeat for the remaining apple halves.

Be sure to cook apples briskly so they do not dissolve into purée

5 With the small knife, peel the skin from the fresh root ginger. With the chef's knife, slice the ginger, cutting across the fibrous grain. Crush each slice with the flat side of the knife, then finely chop the slices.

6 Melt the butter in the large frying pan. Add the apples, ginger, and all but 30 ml (2 tbsp) of the sugar. Sauté, stirring often, until the apples are tender and caramelized, 15–20 minutes. Taste, adding more sugar if needed. Let cool.

HOW TO MAKE PUFF PASTRY DOUGH

Puff pastry dough is the lightest, and yet the richest, of all the pastry doughs. It is composed of literally hundreds of layers of dough interleaved with unsalted butter.

1 Sift the flour onto the work surface and make a well in the centre. Cut 30 ml (2 tbsp) of the butter into pieces and add to the well with the salt, lemon juice, and water.

2 Quickly blend the butter, salt, lemon juice, and water together in the well with your fingertips.

3 Gradually draw in the flour, working with your fingertips to form coarse crumbs. If the crumbs seem dry, add a little more water to form a dough.

4 With a pastry scraper, cut and turn the dough several times until it forms a rough, slightly moist ball.

ANNE SAYS
"At this stage, try to handle the dough as little as possible."

Work with pastry scraper rather than hands, so dough remains cool

5 Score the dough with the pastry scraper to prevent shrinkage; then wrap and chill, 15 minutes.

6 Lightly flour the remaining butter. Pound the butter with a rolling pin, folding and pounding it until it is softened and pliable.

ANNE SAYS
"The butter should be pounded until it is the same consistency as the dough, making it easy to roll them together."

7 With the pastry scraper, shape the piece of butter into a 12.5 cm (5 inch) square.

After pounding, butter is easy to shape

Wrap dough closely around butter

8 Roll out the chilled dough on a lightly floured work surface to a 25 cm (10 inch) square that is slightly thicker in the centre than at the sides.

9 Set the square of butter diagonally in the centre, and pull the corners of the dough around the butter to wrap it like an envelope. Pinch the edges together with your fingers to seal them.

10 Lightly flour the work surface again and turn the dough and butter package over onto it, seam-side down. Tap the package several times with the rolling pin, so that it becomes flattened.

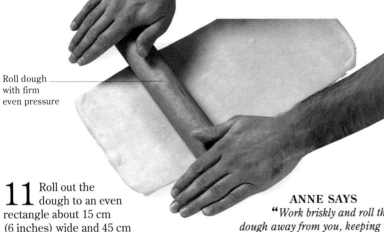

Roll dough with firm even pressure

11 Roll out the dough to an even rectangle about 15 cm (6 inches) wide and 45 cm (18 inches) long.

ANNE SAYS
"Work briskly and roll the dough away from you, keeping it moving on the floured surface."

12 Neatly fold the dough into three, bringing the top third down, and the bottom third up, like a business letter, so that it forms a square of dough.

13 Turn the dough square 90° to bring the seam-side to your right. Gently press the layered ends with the rolling pin to seal them. This completes the first turn. Repeat steps, 11, 12, and 13 to complete a second turn.

ANNE SAYS
"Each rolling out, folding, and pressing of the pastry dough is called a turn."

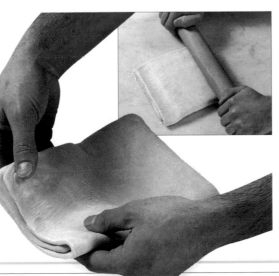

14 Mark the number of turns in one corner of the dough with your fingertips. Wrap the dough and chill, 15 minutes. Repeat 2 turns twice more to make a total of 6 turns, chilling the dough after each set of 2 turns, 15 minutes.

2 ASSEMBLE AND BAKE THE JALOUSIE

1 Sprinkle the baking sheet with cold water. Lightly flour the work surface, then roll out the dough and trim it into a 28 x 32 cm (11 x 13 inch) rectangle with the chef's knife.

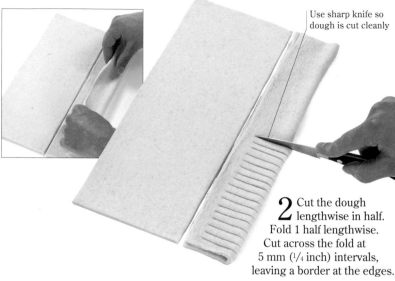

Use sharp knife so dough is cut cleanly

2 Cut the dough lengthwise in half. Fold 1 half lengthwise. Cut across the fold at 5 mm (¼ inch) intervals, leaving a border at the edges.

3 Transfer the uncut rectangle of dough to the prepared baking sheet and press it down lightly. Spoon the apple filling evenly down the centre, leaving a 2 cm (¾ inch) border.

4 Using the pastry brush, moisten the border of the dough with cold water.

Brush border of dough with water so lid can be sealed firmly to base

5 Line up 1 long edge of the slashed dough rectangle with 1 long edge of the rectangle on the baking sheet. Unfold the slashed dough over the filling.

When adding top layer of dough, match each edge carefully to base

6 Press the dough edges together with your fingertips. With a sharp knife, trim the edges to neaten them.

7 Holding the dough in place with one fingertip, scallop the edges at close intervals with the back of the small knife. Chill the jalousie, 15 minutes. Heat the oven to 220°C (425°F, Gas 7). Bake in the oven until puffed and light brown, 20–25 minutes. Meanwhile, whisk the egg white just until it is frothy.

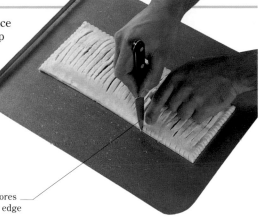

Back of small knife scores without cutting pastry edge

8 Brush the hot jalousie with the egg white and sprinkle the remaining sugar evenly over the top through the small sieve. Return the jalousie to the oven and continue baking until the sugar glaze is crisp and the pastry is deep golden, 10–15 minutes longer. Transfer the jalousie to the wire rack, and let cool.

🍴 TO SERVE

Cut the jalousie crosswise into 6–8 slices and transfer to individual plates. Serve the slices warm or at room temperature.

Crispy glaze comes from egg white and sugar

Caramelized apples are a delicious filling for puff pastry

VARIATION

BANANA SHUTTLES

These pastries are called shuttles because they resemble the tools used by weavers at the loom.

1 Omit the apples and ginger. Make and chill the puff pastry as directed.
2 Combine 50 g (1¾ oz) sugar with 1.25 ml (¼ tsp) each ground cinnamon and ground cloves. Transfer the mixture to a sheet of greaseproof paper. Pour 45 ml (3 tbsp) dark rum into a shallow dish. Peel 3 medium bananas and cut each one crosswise in half. Dip each banana half in the rum, then coat with the sugar mixture.
3 Sprinkle a baking sheet with water. Roll out the puff pastry dough and trim it to a 30 x 37 cm (12 x 15 inch) rectangle. Cut the dough into twelve 7.5 x 12 cm (3 x 5 inch) rectangles. Fold 6 of the rectangles in half lengthwise, and make three 1.25 cm (½ inch) cuts across the fold of each one. Set the remaining rectangles on the baking sheet, pressing lightly.
4 Cut each banana half into thin crosswise slices; then set the slices in the centre of each puff pastry rectangle, leaving a 1 cm (³⁄₈ inch) border around the edge. Brush the dough borders with cold water.
5 Line up and unfold the slashed rectangles over the filled bases. Press the dough edges with your fingertips to seal. Trim one end of each rectangle to a blunt point. Scallop the edges of the shuttles with the back of a small knife.
6 Chill the shuttles, 15 minutes, and bake them in the heated oven as directed, allowing 15–20 minutes before adding the glaze, then bake 10–15 minutes longer.

HAZELNUT, CHOCOLATE, AND ORANGE TART

🍽 SERVES 6–8 🥣 WORK TIME 45–50 MINUTES* ♨ BAKING TIME 35–40 MINUTES

EQUIPMENT

wooden spoon

chef's knife

pastry brush

food processor †

palette knife

greaseproof paper

23 cm (9 inch) flan tin with removable base

wire rack

grater

rolling pin

saucepans

electric mixer ‡

baking sheet

tea towel

pastry scraper

bowls

sieve

small knife

vegetable peeler

metal skewer

† rotary grater can also be used
‡ wooden spoon can also be used

Pasta frolla, the Italian sweet pie pastry, acts as a container for a rich filling, flavoured with ground hazelnuts, plain chocolate, and candied orange zest, topped with a chocolate glaze.

*plus 45 minutes chilling time

INGREDIENTS

oranges

Grand Marnier †

caster sugar

hazelnuts

unsalted butter

plain flour

plain chocolate

eggs

egg yolks

† another orange-flavoured liqueur can also be used

metric	SHOPPING LIST	imperial
2	oranges	2
150 g	caster sugar	5 oz
60 ml	water	2 fl oz
125 g	hazelnuts	4 oz
60 g	plain chocolate	2 oz
150 g	unsalted butter	5 oz
10 ml	plain flour	2 tsp
2	egg yolks	2
1	egg	1
For the pasta frolla dough		
1	orange	1
150 g	plain flour, more if needed	5 oz
75 g	unsalted butter, more for flan tin	2¹/₂ oz
50 g	caster sugar	1³/₄ oz
1.25 ml	salt	¹/₄ tsp
1	egg	1
For the chocolate glaze		
125 g	plain chocolate	4 oz
75 g	unsalted butter	2¹/₂ oz
10 ml	Grand Marnier	2 tsp

ORDER OF WORK

1 MAKE THE PASTA FROLLA DOUGH

2 LINE THE FLAN TIN

3 MAKE THE FILLING; BAKE THE TART

4 MAKE THE CHOCOLATE GLAZE; FINISH THE TART

1 MAKE THE PASTA FROLLA DOUGH

1 Grate the zest from the orange. Sift the flour onto the work surface and make a well in the centre.

Orange zest will flavour dough

2 Pound the butter with the rolling pin to soften it so that it blends in easily with the other ingredients.

3 Put the softened butter, sugar, salt, orange zest, and egg into the well.

Softened butter blends easily with other ingredients

Egg will bind dough together

Fingertips gradually mix flour into wet ingredients

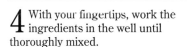

4 With your fingertips, work the ingredients in the well until thoroughly mixed.

5 Draw in the flour with the pastry scraper, then work the flour into the other ingredients with your fingertips until coarse crumbs form. Press the dough into a ball. If it is sticky, work in a little more flour.

6 Lightly flour the work surface. Blend the dough by pushing it away from you with the heel of your hand, then gathering it up, until it is very smooth and peels away from the work surface in one piece, 1–2 minutes.

7 Shape the dough into a ball, wrap it tightly, and chill until firm, about 30 minutes.

Blended dough peels away in one piece

2 LINE THE FLAN TIN

1 Brush the tin with melted butter. Lightly flour the work surface, and roll out the dough into a 28 cm (11 inch) round. Wrap it around the rolling pin, and drape it over the tin.

2 Gently lift the edge of the dough with one hand, and press it well into the bottom of the tin with the other hand, pressing to seal any cracks. Overlap the dough slightly inside the rim of the tin so extra dough is left at the edge of the shell.

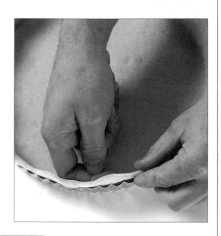

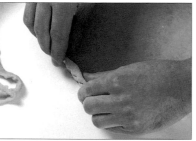

Make fork holes close together

4 Prick the bottom of the pastry shell with a fork to prevent air bubbles forming during cooking. Chill until firm, about 15 minutes.

ANNE SAYS
"The fork holes keep the dough from puffing up during baking."

3 Roll the rolling pin over the top of the tin, pressing down to cut off excess dough. With your thumbs, press the dough evenly up the side of the tin, from the bottom, to increase height of rim.

3 MAKE THE FILLING; BAKE THE TART

Pith is left behind when oranges are carefully pared

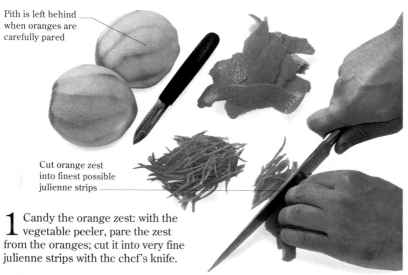

Cut orange zest into finest possible julienne strips

1 Candy the orange zest: with the vegetable peeler, pare the zest from the oranges; cut it into very fine julienne strips with the chef's knife.

2 Bring a small saucepan of water to a boil, add the strips of orange zest, and simmer, 2 minutes. Drain the strips in the sieve; set them aside.

HOW TO TOAST AND SKIN NUTS

Toasting nuts intensifies their flavour and adds crunch to their texture. It also makes it easier to remove thin skin from nuts such as hazelnuts. You can tell that they are toasted when the skins start to pop and the nuts smell fragrant.

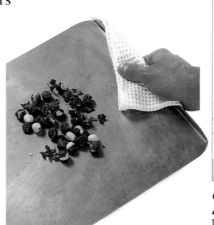

1 Heat the oven to 180°C (350°F, Gas 4). Spread out the nuts on a baking sheet, and toast in the heated oven until they are lightly browned, 6–15 minutes, depending on whether they are whole or chopped, and on the type of nut. Stir occasionally, so they colour evenly.

2 To remove skins from hazelnuts, rub in a tea towel while still hot. Discard the skins. Let cool.

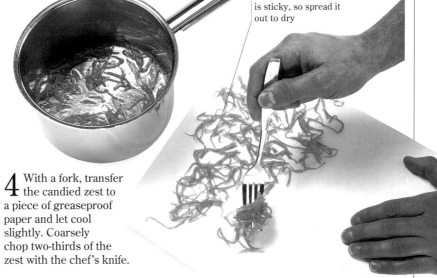

Candied orange zest is sticky, so spread it out to dry

3 Put one-third of the sugar into a pan, add the measured water, and heat gently until dissolved, shaking the pan once or twice. Add the zest strips, and simmer until all the water has evaporated, and the zest strips are transparent and tender, 8–10 minutes.

4 With a fork, transfer the candied zest to a piece of greaseproof paper and let cool slightly. Coarsely chop two-thirds of the zest with the chef's knife.

5 Toast and skin the hazelnuts (see box, above). Let cool. Leave the oven temperature at 180°C (350°F, Gas 4), and put in the baking sheet to heat. Cut the chocolate into chunks, then finely chop with the chef's knife. Or, chop it in the food processor.

6 Put the remaining sugar in the food processor, add the hazelnuts, and finely grind. Or, grind just the nuts in a rotary grater and mix with the sugar.

ANNE SAYS
"The sugar helps prevent the hazelnuts becoming oily."

Finely chopped chocolate will be evenly distributed in tart filling

7 Beat the butter until creamy. Add the flour and the hazelnut mixture, and continue beating until light and fluffy, 2–3 minutes. Add the yolks and egg, one at a time, beating after each addition. Mix in the chocolate and chopped candied orange zest.

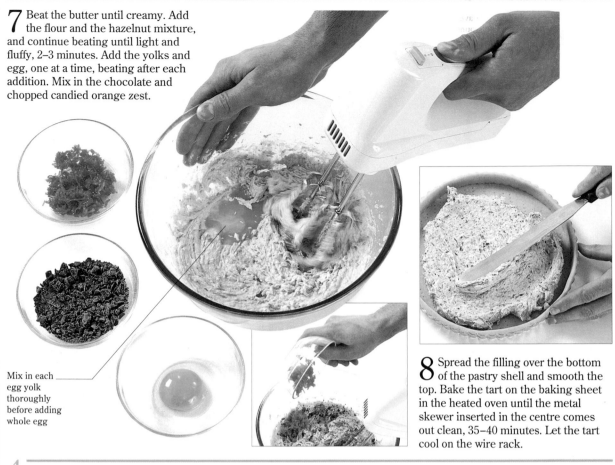

Mix in each egg yolk thoroughly before adding whole egg

8 Spread the filling over the bottom of the pastry shell and smooth the top. Bake the tart on the baking sheet in the heated oven until the metal skewer inserted in the centre comes out clean, 35–40 minutes. Let the tart cool on the wire rack.

4 MAKE THE CHOCOLATE GLAZE; FINISH THE TART

1 While the tart is cooling, make the chocolate glaze. Cut the chocolate into chunks. Heat the chocolate in a bowl set over a saucepan of hot water, stirring occasionally, just until melted.

Butter gives glaze glossy finish when spread on tart

2 Cut the butter into small pieces and gently stir it into the warm melted chocolate in 2–3 batches.

3 Add the Grand Marnier and stir it into the chocolate mixture, adding more to taste. Let the glaze cool to tepid. Set the flan tin on a bowl to loosen and remove the side.

Leave border around glaze for decoration of candied zest

4 Pour the glaze onto the tart, and spread it smoothly over the centre. With the edge of the palette knife, carefully mark radiating lines in the glaze, holding the knife in one hand and turning the tart with the other.

🍽 TO SERVE
Slide the tart from the tin base onto a plate. Decorate with the remaining candied orange zest. Cut the tart into wedges and serve at room temperature.

VARIATION
CHOCOLATE AND WALNUT TRUFFLE TART

In this version of Hazelnut, Chocolate, and Orange Tart, toasted walnuts take the place of hazelnuts in the filling – and some of them are reserved and coated in melted chocolate to decorate the tart. A topping of cocoa powder is sifted over the glazed tart to echo the coating for chocolate truffles.

1 Omit the hazelnuts, orange zest, sugar for candying, and candied orange zest. Make the pasta frolla dough, without the zest, and chill as directed. Line the flan tin and chill the pastry shell as directed.

Orange and chocolate are a classic flavour combination

2 Toast 150 g (5 oz) walnut halves as for the hazelnuts, but do not skin them. Reserve 8 halves. Grind the remaining nuts with 100 g (3½ oz) sugar as directed. Make the filling as directed, adding 5 ml (1 tsp) vanilla essence in place of the candied orange zest.
3 Bake the tart as directed and let cool. Melt 175 g (6 oz) plain chocolate as directed for the glaze. Dip the reserved walnut halves into the melted chocolate to coat completely; set aside.
4 Finish the glaze as directed, using the remaining melted chocolate. Glaze the top of the tart completely, without marking it in a pattern. Let cool.
5 Just before serving, sift 30–45 ml (2–3 tbsp) cocoa powder in a generous layer over the tart. Arrange the chocolate-coated walnut halves on top of the tart. Cut it into wedges and serve at room temperature.

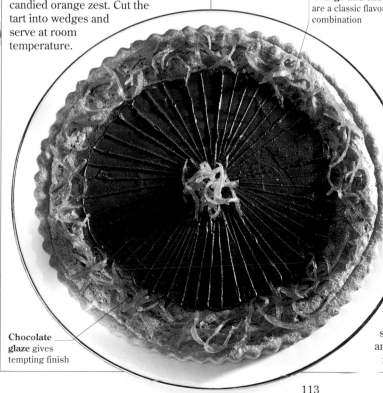

Chocolate **glaze** gives tempting finish

GETTING AHEAD
The dough can be made up to 2 days ahead and kept, tightly wrapped, in the refrigerator. The tart can be baked and stored up to 2 days in an airtight container, and the flavours will mellow. Add the glaze not more than 4 hours before serving.

PISTACHIO AND RICOTTA PHYLLO PIE

🍳 SERVES 6–8   🥣 WORK TIME 35–40 MINUTES   ♨ BAKING TIME 45–50 MINUTES

EQUIPMENT

pastry brush

kitchen scissors

food processor †

small knife

bowls

electric mixer ‡

aluminium foil

grater

20 cm (8 inch) square cake tin

small brush

rubber spatula

baking sheet

wire rack

saucepans

tea towels

† blender can also be used
‡ hand whisk can also be used

Phyllo pastry can be used to make many different shapes. Here, a giant box of layered phyllo dough is filled with layers of ricotta cheese and ground pistachios, and finished with phyllo rosettes.

GETTING AHEAD
The baked pie can be kept in the refrigerator up to 2 days; allow it to come to room temperature before serving.

metric	SHOPPING LIST	imperial
500 g	package phyllo dough	1 lb
125 g	unsalted butter, more for cake tin	4 oz
For the pistachio and ricotta fillings		
90 g	shelled pistachio nuts	3 oz
45 ml	caster sugar	3 tbsp
45 ml	light soft brown sugar	3 tbsp
2	lemons	2
1	egg	1
175 g	ricotta cheese	6 oz
75 ml	soured cream	2 1/2 fl oz
5 ml	vanilla essence	1 tsp
30 ml	honey	2 tbsp
10 ml	plain flour	2 tsp
	salt	
45 g	raisins	1 1/2 oz
For the topping		
5 ml	ground cinnamon	1 tsp
15 ml	caster sugar	1 tbsp

INGREDIENTS

ricotta cheese

shelled pistachio nuts

phyllo dough

ground cinnamon

soured cream

vanilla essence

soft brown sugar

plain flour

unsalted butter

raisins

honey

sugar

egg

lemons

ANNE SAYS
"About 10 sheets of phyllo dough are needed for this recipe, but I always have a few extra in case some tear. Any remaining sheets can be wrapped tightly and frozen."

ORDER OF WORK

1 MAKE THE PISTACHIO AND RICOTTA FILLINGS

2 ASSEMBLE AND BAKE THE PIE

1 MAKE THE PISTACHIO AND RICOTTA FILLINGS

Grinding pistachios with sugar helps keep them from turning to paste

1 Melt the butter in a saucepan. In the food processor, coarsely chop the pistachio nuts. Add the sugars and work the nuts until finely chopped, 1 minute longer. While the blade is turning, add 15 ml (1 tbsp) of the melted butter and work until coarse crumbs form.

2 Finely grate the zest from each of the lemons, using the small brush to remove any zest remaining on the grater. Set aside. In a medium bowl, stir the egg. Add the ricotta cheese.

Filling combines classic Mediterranean ingredients

Honey is easier to measure if it is warmed first

3 Beat the egg and ricotta cheese with the electric mixer, or with a hand whisk, until smooth.

4 Add the soured cream, lemon zest, vanilla essence, honey, flour, and a pinch of salt to the egg and ricotta mixture. Continue beating until light and fluffy, 2–3 minutes. Stir in the raisins.

2 ASSEMBLE AND BAKE THE PIE

1 Heat the oven to 180°C (350°F, Gas 4). Put the baking sheet in the oven to heat. Brush the cake tin with melted butter; line with a strip of double thickness foil, draping excess over edges. Roll up the excess to form handles. Brush with melted butter.

2 Lay a tea towel on the work surface and sprinkle it lightly with water. Unroll the phyllo dough sheets onto it. Trim the sheets to 20 x 40 cm (8 x 16 inch) rectangles. Cover the sheets and trimmings with a second dampened tea towel.

Melted butter is essential in composition of pie

3 Put 1 of the sheets of dough on top of a third dampened tea towel and brush with butter. Lay it in the bottom of the tin so that part of the sheet drapes over one edge of the tin.

4 Butter a second sheet. Lay it in the bottom of the tin so that part drapes over the edge at right angles to the first sheet. Butter third and fourth sheets, laying and pressing them into the tin so the excess drapes over the remaining 2 sides. Cut the remaining sheets in half to make 20 cm (8 inch) squares; cover with the dampened tea towel.

Handle dough carefully so it does not tear

5 With the rubber spatula, spread half of the ricotta cheese filling evenly over the dough in the tin.

6 Butter 3 of the squares of phyllo dough and lay each one, butter-side up, over the filling in the tin.

7 Evenly distribute half of the nut mixture on top of the buttered dough.

Overhanging dough will be folded over filling to seal it in

Make sure nut mixture is evenly spread over dough

8 Butter and layer 3 more squares of dough on top of the nut mixture. Layer the remaining cheese and nut fillings with the buttered phyllo dough, finishing the layering with 3 squares of buttered dough.

9 Fold the 4 overhanging pieces of dough over the pie and brush the top with butter. Cut the reserved trimmings into 5 cm (2 inch) wide strips.

10 Curl the strips to form loose rosettes and arrange on top of the pie. Combine the cinnamon and sugar in a small bowl.

11 Brush pie and rosettes with the remaining melted butter, and sprinkle the cinnamon and sugar over the top. Bake on the heated baking sheet until golden brown and flaky, and a metal skewer inserted into the centre for 30 seconds is hot to the touch, 45–50 minutes. Let cool slightly in the tin. Transfer to the wire rack; let cool to room temperature. Discard the foil.

🍴 TO SERVE

Transfer the pie to a serving plate. Cut it into squares for serving, and set on individual plates.

Phyllo pastry contains crunchy nuts and smooth ricotta with juicy raisins

Crisp rosettes are an appealing finish

V A R I A T I O N

POPPY SEED PHYLLO PIE

Poppy seeds replace pistachios in this round phyllo pie.

1 Omit the pistachio filling, and cinnamon and sugar topping. Make the ricotta cheese filling as directed.
2 Put 60 g (2 oz) poppy seeds in a bowl, pour over boiling water to cover, then let stand, 2 minutes. Drain. Reserve 5 ml (1 tsp) poppy seeds for sprinkling. Grind the remainder in a spice or coffee grinder.
3 In a saucepan, combine the ground poppy seeds with 60 ml (2 fl oz) milk. Bring just to a boil and simmer, about 2 minutes. Off the heat, stir in 60 ml (2 fl oz) honey and 45 g (1 1/2 oz) raisins. Transfer to a bowl and let cool. Beat 1 egg to mix; stir into cool filling.
4 Melt the butter. Brush a 23 cm (9 inch) flan tin, with a removable base, with the melted butter. Lay a tea towel on the work surface and sprinkle it lightly with water. Unroll the phyllo dough sheets on top. Trim 4 sheets into 25 x 30 cm (10 x 12 inch) rectangles. Cover, butter, and layer at right angles as directed.
5 Cut the remaining sheets in half, then into 23 cm (9 inch) rounds.
6 Fill and layer the pie as directed. Fold the overhanging pieces of dough over the filling, pleating them into a neat pattern around the edge.
7 Brush with the remaining butter and sprinkle the reserved poppy seeds over the top. Bake as directed.
8 Let cool slightly, then set the tin on a bowl to loosen and remove the side. Slide the pie from the base onto a wire rack. Serve at room temperature.

FRESH FRUIT TARTLETS

EQUIPMENT

bowls

chef's knife

pastry brush

whisk

wire rack

small knife

palette knife

pastry scraper

rolling pin

baking sheets

sieve

saucepans, 1 heavy-based with lid

chopping board

Make the most of fresh colourful fruit in these crisp tartlets. If you wish, you can save 40–50 minutes work time by substituting 1 lb ready-prepared puff pastry dough for the homemade puff pastry dough used in the recipe.
*plus 1¾ hours chilling time

INGREDIENTS

kiwi fruit

plums

papaya

plain flour

lemon juice

caster sugar

egg

egg yolks

kirsch†

unsalted butter

apricot jam

milk

vanilla pod‡

† water can also be used
‡ 5 ml (1 tsp) vanilla essence can also be used

ORDER OF WORK

1 **MAKE THE DOUGH; SHAPE AND BAKE THE TARTLET SHELLS**

2 **MAKE THE PASTRY CREAM**

3 **PREPARE THE FRUIT, MAKE THE GLAZE, AND ASSEMBLE THE TARTLETS**

metric	SHOPPING LIST	imperial
1	small papaya, weighing about 250 g (8 oz)	1
1	medium kiwi fruit	1
2	purple plums, total weight about 125 g (4 oz)	2
2	yellow plums, total weight about 125 g (4 oz)	2
	For the puff pastry dough	
250 g	plain flour	8 oz
250 g	unsalted butter	8 oz
5 ml	salt	1 tsp
5 ml	lemon juice	1 tsp
125 ml	water, more if needed	4 fl oz
1	egg, plus 2.5 ml (½ tsp) salt for glaze	1
	For the pastry cream	
1	vanilla pod	1
500 ml	milk	16 fl oz
6	egg yolks	6
75 g	caster sugar	2½ oz
30 g	plain flour	1 oz
15 ml	unsalted butter	1 tbsp
	For the apricot glaze	
125 ml	apricot jam	4 fl oz
15 ml	kirsch	1 tbsp

1 MAKE THE DOUGH; SHAPE AND BAKE THE TARTLET SHELLS

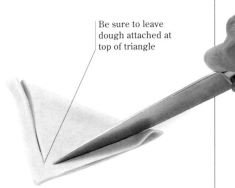

Be sure to leave dough attached at top of triangle

1 Make and chill the dough (see pages 104–105). Make the egg glaze: lightly beat the egg with the salt. Sprinkle a baking sheet with water.

2 Lightly flour the work surface, then roll out the puff pastry dough and trim it to a 37 cm (15 inch) square. With the chef's knife, cut it into nine 12.5 cm (5 inch) squares.

3 Fold 1 square in half to form a triangle. Cut a 1.25 cm (½ inch) border on the 2 unfolded edges of the triangle, leaving the dough attached at the top of the triangle.

Point of border meets opposite point of inner square

4 Transfer the dough triangle to the prepared baking sheet, unfold, and press down lightly. Brush cold water around the edge of the inner square. Pick up a point of the border, lift, and flip it over to the opposite point of the inner square. Repeat with the remaining border so that a twist is formed at 2 corners of the square.

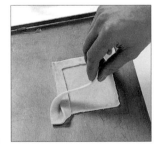

5 With your fingertips, press the border firmly onto the dough beneath. Cut and place the borders for the remaining squares, using more baking sheets as necessary. Mark a "V" pattern on the border of each square with the back of the small knife, and scallop the edges. Prick the bottoms of the shells with a fork.

7 Bake the pastry shells, in batches if necessary, in the heated oven until starting to brown, 10–15 minutes. Reduce the oven temperature to 190°C (375°F, Gas 5), and if the dough has risen in the centre, prick it again and press down with the back of a fork. Continue baking until the pastry is golden and very crisp, 5–10 minutes longer. Transfer to the wire rack to cool.

6 Brush the borders with egg glaze and chill until firm, 15 minutes. Heat the oven to 220°C (425°F, Gas 7).

Bake pastry very thoroughly so it is deep golden

2 MAKE THE PASTRY CREAM

Rub butter over surface of cream with fork

1 Split the vanilla pod, if using. In the heavy-based pan, bring the milk to a boil with the vanilla pod. Remove from the heat, cover, and let stand, 10–15 minutes. Whisk the egg yolks with the sugar until thick and light coloured, 2–3 minutes. Add the flour and stir it in with the whisk.

2 Gradually stir in the hot milk until the mixture is smooth. Pour it back into the saucepan. Bring to a boil over medium heat, whisking constantly until it thickens. Lower the heat and cook the pastry cream, still whisking, until it softens slightly, about 2 minutes, to ensure the flour leaves no aftertaste.

3 Remove the pan from the heat, take out the vanilla pod, if using, or stir in the vanilla essence. Transfer to a bowl, then rub the butter over the surface of the cream to keep it from forming a skin. Chill, 30 minutes.

3 PREPARE THE FRUIT, MAKE THE GLAZE, AND ASSEMBLE THE TARTLETS

Papaya flesh will add vibrant colour to tartlets

Spoon scoops out seeds easily

1 Cut the papaya lengthwise in half. Scoop out seeds. With the small knife, remove the skin; cut the papaya into thin wedges. Cut wedges crosswise in half.

2 Trim off the ends of the kiwi fruit. Set it upright and peel off the skin in strips, working from top to bottom. Cut the fruit across into slices.

3 With the small knife, cut each plum in half, using the indentation on one side as a guide. Twist with both hands to loosen the plum halves; then pull them apart. Scoop out the stone with the point of the knife, and discard. Cut each plum half into thin wedges.

4 Make the glaze: heat the apricot jam with the kirsch in a pan, stirring, just until melted. Work through a sieve; melt again. Brush the bottom of each shell with glaze.

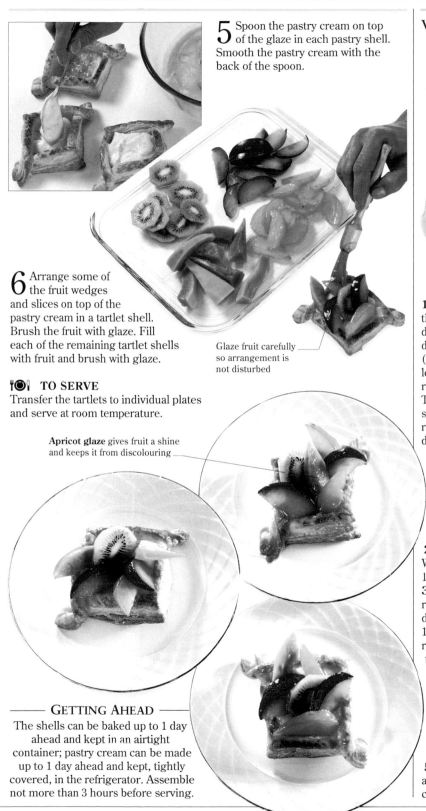

5 Spoon the pastry cream on top of the glaze in each pastry shell. Smooth the pastry cream with the back of the spoon.

6 Arrange some of the fruit wedges and slices on top of the pastry cream in a tartlet shell. Brush the fruit with glaze. Fill each of the remaining tartlet shells with fruit and brush with glaze.

Glaze fruit carefully so arrangement is not disturbed

¶○¶ TO SERVE
Transfer the tartlets to individual plates and serve at room temperature.

Apricot glaze gives fruit a shine and keeps it from discolouring

—— **GETTING AHEAD** ——
The shells can be baked up to 1 day ahead and kept in an airtight container; pastry cream can be made up to 1 day ahead and kept, tightly covered, in the refrigerator. Assemble not more than 3 hours before serving.

V A R I A T I O N
MIXED BERRY TART
Here, the puff pastry dough is rolled out into a long strip that is filled with Grand Marnier-flavoured pastry cream and topped with a trio of fresh berries arranged in long lines.

1 Make and chill the puff pastry dough as directed. Roll out half of the dough and trim it to a 15 x 35 cm (6 x 14 inch) rectangle, or to the full length of your baking sheet. (Keep the remaining dough for another use.) Trim the edges. Cut a 2 cm (³/₄ inch) strip from each long side of the rectangle. Transfer the rectangle to a dampened baking sheet. Brush cold water along a 2.5 cm (1 inch) border on each long edge of the rectangle, and set the strips on top to frame the edges. Brush the bottom of the rectangle and the frame with egg glaze. Chill, and bake the pastry shell as directed.
2 Make the pastry cream as directed. When the pastry cream is cool, stir in 15–30 ml (1–2 tbsp) Grand Marnier.
3 Make the glaze as directed, using redcurrant jelly in place of apricot jam; do not work through a sieve. Pick over 175 g (6 oz) each of strawberries, raspberries, and blueberries, washing them only if dirty. Halve the strawberries if large.
4 Brush the bottom of the pastry shell with the redcurrant glaze, and spoon the pastry cream on top of the glaze. Arrange the mixed berries lengthwise in lines on top of the pastry cream and brush with glaze.
5 Transfer the tart to a serving platter and serve at room temperature, cut crosswise into slices.

PIES AND TARTS KNOW-HOW

No dessert is more appealing than a home-baked pie or tart. To make the most of your time in the kitchen, plan ahead. Be sure to check the section on "Getting Ahead" in each recipe because many preparations can be taken care of well in advance. Set aside time to find the finest and freshest ingredients. The quality and flavour of each ingredient – from the best chocolate to sun-ripened fruit – contribute to the success of your culinary efforts.

CHOOSING

The occasion is the first factor to consider when choosing an appropriate pie or tart. For a buffet, I like to make a selection of pies and tarts so that guests may choose their favourites. Recipes with contrasting colours and textures, such as Hazelnut, Chocolate, and Orange Tart, Pistachio and Ricotta Phyllo Pie, Lime and Cardamom Tart, and Mixed Berry Tart, are ideal, and they can either be cut into neat slices or squares. Every family loves Traditional Apple Pie, so serve it hot to end a casual supper at home, topped with a scoop of ice cream. Mississippi Mud Pie, with swirls of fudge sauce, is sure to please any chocolate lover. For more formal dinners, Flaky Pear Tartlets, Apple Jalousie, or Caramelized Upside-Down Mango Tartlets are appropriate.

The time of year is also a consideration – baking with the best a season offers is always a good idea. Late spring marks the start of the stone-fruit season, with cherries being some of the first to ripen. Cherry Tartlets is the perfect recipe for big, beautiful cherries. From the summer time garden, there are baskets of berries and peaches. Show them off with plain and fancy favourites like Bavarian Blueberry Tart, Peach Pie with Walnut Pastry, and Fresh Fruit Tartlets. Naturally, autumn is the perfect season to bake Amelia Simmons' Pumpkin Pie. And when the cold winter months arrive, Fresh Mincemeat Tart served with whisky butter, Fig and Mulled Wine Tart, and Triple-Decker Prune Tart are delicious – especially by the fire with family and friends.

DECORATING AND PRESENTING

Just a small decorative touch on a pie or tart can make all the difference; for example, a quick sprinkling of icing sugar, or a golden brushing of egg glaze. In each recipe you will see how to neaten and decorate pastry edges, or how to dress up the top with shapes cut from pastry trimmings. Included are instructions on how to shape a pastry rose, how to create a lattice topping, how to make maple-leaf shapes, and how to make an impressive pastry plait.

Before baking a pie, I always think about how it will look on the table, and then try to choose an attractive dish. I put pie dishes on carefully chosen platters – rustic, elegant, or contemporary, depending on the occasion. When serving a pie or tart on a buffet table set with a number of other dishes, you can use a cake stand so the pie is raised. There are many attractive glass and china stands available, both new and antique.

An important factor when serving pies and tarts is temperature. The flavour of creamy fillings and aromatic fruit pies can vary significantly, depending on whether they are served chilled or at room temperature.

Pies and tarts can be served plain or with a number of accompaniments. You will find that I've made many suggestions in this book for appropriate sauces, creams, or ice creams. A sauce may be as simple as a fruit purée, such as the mango coulis served with Caramelized Upside-Down Mango Tartlets. The whisky butter that I suggest serving with Fresh Mincemeat Tart takes only a little more time to prepare, and works very well with a warm tart like this. Crème fraîche pairs nicely with a rich recipe like Pear Pie with Walnut Pastry. Sweetened, flavoured whipped cream (Chantilly cream) is the perfect foil for the fruit- or nut-filled pies – Classic Pecan Pie is a good example. And of course there is ice cream. Pies and tarts served with ice cream are an American tradition. Try Peach Pie with Walnut Pastry with a generous scoop of vanilla or your favourite nut-flavoured ice cream, or Triple-Decker Dried Peach Tart with lemon sorbet.

DECORATIVE EDGES

It is surprisingly easy to give your pies and tarts a professional and eye-catching finish. By simply using your fingers, kitchen scissors, or a knife, you can shape or snip the pastry dough edge into the decoration of your choice. The edges illustrated here are just three examples of the possible decorative edges.

SCALLOPED EDGE	FLUTED EDGE	FEATHERED EDGE

Double crusted pies are ideal for making a scalloped edge; the double layer of pastry dough is easy to pinch into a neat decoration, and it catches juice that may seep from the pie filling.

The edge of a single crusted pie is built up so that it can be shaped into the decoration of your choice. Here, a quick pinch with your thumbs will transform plain pastry dough into an attractive fluted design.

For a more elegant finish, snip the pastry dough with a pair of kitchen scissors. The feathered edge is delicate after baking, so handle the finished pie carefully to keep the pastry intact.

1 With a small knife, trim the top crust even with the bottom crust. Press the edges together to seal them.

2 Place the forefinger of one hand on the edge of the dough, pointing outwards. With the forefinger and thumb of your other hand, push the dough inwards to form a scallop. Continue around the edge of the shell in this way until the scalloping is completed.

1 Fold under the excess dough at the edge of the shell, then bring up above the pie dish rim to make an edge with a double thickness of dough.

2 Lightly press your thumbs together diagonally into the edge of the dough to make a ridge. Continue around the edge of the shell in this way until the fluting is completed.

1 Pinch the dough edge between your thumb and forefinger so it stands up. With scissors, make 1.25 cm (½ inch) diagonal cuts at 1.25 cm (½ inch) intervals around the edge of the shell.

2 With your fingertips, push one point towards the centre of the shell, and the next point towards the edge of the shell. Continue around the edge of the shell in this way until the feathering is completed.

TECHNIQUES

In this volume, you can learn how to make 11 different pastries – British shortcrust pastry and its counterpart, light American-style pie pastry, are among them. French pâte brisée is thin yet robust, with a crumbly sweet version called pâte sucrée. You'll find orange-flavoured Italian pasta frolla, several nut pastries, crisply layered puff pastry, buttery brioche yeast dough, and an unusual pastry containing cornmeal. You will become accomplished at lining pie dishes and flan tins so the pastry dough does not shrink.

The tins I have chosen for these pies and tarts vary in shape and size. When lining a tin with pastry dough, it is important to use the proper technique. Stretching the dough can cause it to shrink during baking. When shaped correctly, the dough will not shrink or slide down the side of the tin. The method used for lining straight-sided French-style flan tins varies slightly from the technique we suggest for sloping-sided pie dishes. For both, quick and careful handling of the dough is mandatory if the finished pastry is to be light. For pies and tarts with a moist filling, the pastry shell is often partially baked before the filling is added to prevent the dough becoming soggy. In some cases, the shell is completely baked before the filling is added. This step, which is called baking blind, is standard for both pies and tarts. Instructions are given for lining and weighing down the pastry shell so the dough keeps its shape while baking blind. One last caution, be sure to chill the pastry shell thoroughly before it goes into the oven.

Adding decorations to your pies and tarts will become second nature, as will a brushing of glaze or a sprinkling of sugar. I've included instructions for simple edges, such

as marking the dough by pressing with the tines of a fork or the edge of a spoon; you can also crimp and scallop the edge with your fingers, or make an impressive plait from strips of dough. To give pastry lids a lift, you'll see how to make leaves, roses, and berries from dough trimmings. Open tarts may be embellished with a woven pastry lattice, sealed at the edges so the strips do not shrink, or you may add some delicate white chocolate leaves, strawberry fans, or candied lemon slices.

Techniques you will come across when making fillings include preparing fruit, from everyday apples, oranges, and pears to tropical mangoes and fresh figs, toasting and chopping nuts, and melting chocolate and gelatine.

The secrets of smooth lemon curd and lump-free pastry cream will be revealed, and cloud-like meringue need never again be out of your reach. I will show you how to make coffee ice cream and how to dress it up with swirls of fudge sauce and chopped nuts. You will see how simple it can be to make golden caramel sauce and smooth mango coulis – delicious with an assortment of desserts.

GETTING AHEAD

Pastry doughs benefit from being made ahead. All need to rest in the refrigerator at least 15 minutes before they are rolled out, and, if tightly wrapped, they can be refrigerated up to 2 days, or frozen up to 3 months. Puff pastry should be taken to 4 "turns" before storage, then turned twice more just before using. Let the dough come almost to room temperature before rolling it out.

You may find it easier to roll out and shape dough before storage, and in this case it can be baked straight from the refrigerator. If freezing shaped pastry shells, lids, or shapes, freeze them in the dish or tin or on the baking sheet until hard, then unmould, and wrap them tightly. Defrost them, 1–2 hours, in the refrigerator before baking.

Freshly baked pastry is incomparable, but pie shells made of richer dough, such as puff pastry or pâte sucrée, can be kept, 1–2 days, in an airtight container without harm.

How long you can keep a finished pie depends very much on the filling. A moist filling of custard or fresh fruit can soften even crisply baked pastry within an hour or two. However, a tart with a firmer filling, such as Hazelnut, Chocolate, and Orange Tart, holds well, up to 2 days. You'll find instructions for getting ahead with each recipe.

MICROWAVE COOKING

Baking pastry is not one of the strong points of a microwave oven. However, it can be used for cooking the crumb crusts of Mississippi Mud Pie and Gingernut Ice Cream Pie, and the almond crust of Chocolate Pye with a Crunchy Crust and its variations.

A microwave oven can also help speed the melting of chocolate and gelatine. Medium power is recommended for melting chocolate, and timing depends on the output of your microwave oven, the type, and the amount of chocolate. For instance, 60 g (2 oz) chopped plain chocolate takes about 2 minutes on Medium (50% power). Nuts, such as almonds, hazelnuts, and walnuts, and desiccated coconut can be toasted on High (100% power). Use the microwave, too, to melt butter for brushing your pie dishes and flan tins.

HOW-TO BOXES

In **Perfect Pies and Tarts** *you'll find pictures of all the techniques used in the recipes. However, some basic preparations appear in a number of recipes in special "how-to" boxes:*

INDEX

ACKNOWLEDGMENTS

Photographers David Murray
Jules Selmes
Photographer's Assistant Stephen Head

Chef Eric Treuille
Cookery Consultant Martha Holmberg
Home Economist Sarah Lowman

Reader Lisa Minsky

Typesetting Linda Parker
Text film by Disc to Print (UK) Ltd

Production Consultant Lorraine Baird

*Carroll and Brown Limited would like to
thank Magimix (UK) Limited, who supplied
the Cuisine Systeme food processor, and
Corning Limited, who supplied the Pyrex
cookware.*

*Anne Willan would like to thank her
chief editor Hilaire Walden and
associate editor Jacqueline Bobrow for
their vital help with writing the book
and researching and testing the
recipes, aided by Jane Reilly,
Joanna Rend, and La Varenne's
chefs and trainees.*

NOTES

- Metric and imperial measures have been calculated separately. Only use one set of measures as they are not exact equivalents.

- All spoon measurements are level.

- Spoon measurements are calculated using a standard 5 ml teaspoon and 15 ml tablespoon to give an accurate measurement of small amounts.